Yellow Pencils

Yellow Pencils

Contemporary Poetry
by New Zealand Women

Chosen by Lydia Wevers

Auckland
Oxford University Press
Melbourne   Oxford   New York

Oxford University Press
Oxford University Press, Walton Street, Oxford OX2 6DP

OXFORD   NEW YORK   TORONTO
DELHI   BOMBAY   CALCUTTA   MADRAS   KARACHI
PETALING JAYA   SINGAPORE   HONG KONG   TOKYO
NAIROBI   DAR ES SALAAM   CAPE TOWN
MELBOURNE   AUCKLAND
and associated companies in
BERLIN and IBADAN

Oxford is a trade mark of Oxford University Press

First published 1988
Introduction and selection © Lydia Wevers 1988

ISBN 0 19 558178 4

Photoset in Palatino by Rennies Illustrations Ltd.,
Printed in Australia by Australian Print Group
Published by Oxford University Press
1A Matai Road, Greenlane, Auckland 3, New Zealand

Contents

Helen Jacobs, (Elaine Jakobsson)

Born 1929 in Patea, Taranaki and now lives in Eastbourne, Wellington.
Her occupations have included teaching, Play Centre Supervisor and
Director of Training, Mayor of Eastbourne 1980-1986, and she is now

a member of the Planning Tribunal in the Justice Department. Her publications include *A Place to Play* and *An Approach to Playgrounds*, and a book of poems, *This Cording, This Artery*, 1984.

Judith Lonie

Born in Brisbane, Australia 1935 and died 18 December 1982. She gained a degree in Classics from Sydney University and taught in schools in New South Wales for twelve years and in the English Department at Otago University for one year. At the time of her death she had completed a BSc Hons in Speech Therapy at the University of Newcastle upon Tyne in England. She published *Earth into Moon*, 1971.

Meg Campbell

Born 1937 at Palmerston North and now lives at Pukerua Bay. She has worked in the National Film Library, Wellington City Library, Whitcoulls' Stationers, and Victoria Book Centre, and is now retired. Her publications include *The Way Back* 1981 and *A Durable Fire* 1982.

Riemke Ensing

Born in 1939 in Groningen, the Netherlands, and now lives in Howick, Auckland. She has taught at the University of Auckland, writes occasionally for *Art NZ*, and gives talks and poetry readings when invited. Her numerous publications include editing the first substantial anthology of New Zealand women poets, *Private Gardens*. She is represented in many anthologies, has published widely in literary magazines in New Zealand

and abroad, and broadcast on radio and television. Her current project is the preparation of an edition of Helen Shaw's essays, articles, and occasional writings for publication.

Rachel McAlpine

Born 1940 in Fairlie, South Canterbury, and now lives in Wellington and Taranaki. She has worked on radio plays, written plays, and novels, as well as poetry. Collections include *Lament for Ariadne*, 1975, *Stay at the Dinner Party*, 1977, *Fancy Dress*, 1978, *House Poems*, 1980, *Recording Angel*, 1983, and the recently published *Selected Poems*, 1988, and her novels are *The Limits of Green*, 1986 and *Running Away From Home*, 1987.

Fiona Kidman

Born March 1940 in Hawera and now lives in Wellington. She is a full-time writer and is currently the Writers' Fellow at Victoria University. She has published poetry, novels, and short stories. Her novel *The Book of Secrets*, 1987, won the fiction section of the New Zealand Book Awards.

Elizabeth Smither

Born 1941 in New Plymouth and is currently still living there. She has
worked as a librarian, journalist, critic, and editor. She has published
numerous poetry collections including *Here Come the Clouds*, 1975, *You're
Very Seductive William Carlos Williams*, 1978, *The Legend of Marcello Mastroianni's
Wife*, 1981, *Casanova's ankles*, 1983, *Shakespeare Virgins*, 1983, *Professor Musgrove's
Canary*, 1985, and *Gorilla/Guerilla*, 1986, she has also published novels and
a children's book.

Sue Harlen

Born in 1942, she is currently working for VSA as a teacher trainer
in Thailand. She has published *Hook Hours*, 1985.

Heather McPherson

Born 1942 in Tauranga and now resides in Matata. She has published
A Figurehead, a Face, 1982, and *The Third Myth*, 1986.

Christina Conrad (Beere)

Born 1942 at Te Marua, Hutt Valley. She lives at Waiuku, South Auckland. She is a painter and poet.

Dinah Hawken

Born 1943 in Hawera and now lives in Wellington. She is a student counsellor at Victoria University and also runs therapy groups for women. She has published *It Has No Sound and is Blue*, 1987.

Joanna Paul

Born in 1945 in Hamilton, she now lives in Wanganui. She is a painter, poet, photographer, and film maker. She has published a number of books, including *Imogen*, a collection of poems, and has had poetry published in *Morepork*, *Parallax*, and *Islands*.

Fiona Farrell Poole

Born 1947 in Oamaru. She lives in Palmerston North and works as a teacher at a secondary school and as a writer. She has published plays, short stories, and a radio play. *Cutting Out* was published in 1987.

Keri Hulme

Born 1947 in Christchurch, she now lives at Okarito, Westland. She is of Kai Tahu descent, affiliated to Kati Rakiamoa and Ka Ruahikihiki. She works at fishing and writing. She has written poetry, stories, and novels, and has published *The Silences Between [Moeraki Conversations]* 1982, *The Bone People* 1984, *Lost Possessions* 1985, and *Te Kaihau/The Windeaters*, 1986.

Vivienne Joseph

Born in 1948 in Wellington, she now lives in Stokes Valley. She has published *A Desirable Property*, 1985.

Jan Kemp

Born 1949 in Hamilton, and now lives in Singapore. She is a teacher of English as a foreign language, presently employed at the National University of Singapore. Her publications include *Against the Softness of Woman*, 1976, *Diamonds and Gravel*, 1979, *Ice-Breaker Poems*, 1980, and *Five Poems*, 1988.

Cilla McQueen

Born 1949 in Birmingham, England, she now lives in Dunedin. She works full-time as a poet and her publications are *Homing In*, 1982, *Anti-Gravity*, 1984, *Wild Sweets*, 1986, and *Benzina*, 1988. McQueen has published poetry in major New Zealand and overseas literary magazines.

Janet Charman

Born 1954 in Auckland, she now works as a receptionist. She has recently published *Two Deaths in One Night*, 1987.

Anne French

Born 1956 in Wellington, now lives in Auckland. She is Managing Editor of Oxford University Press and has published *All Cretans are Liars*, 1987 and *The Male as Evader*, 1988.

Michele Leggott

Born 1956, she now lives in Devonport, Auckland, and teaches part-time at Auckland University. Her poetry has been published in *Broadsheet, Craccum, Kiwi, Islands, Landfall, Rambling Jack*, and *Untold*. She has a publication forthcoming from John Hopkins University Press and has edited the poetry selection for *Landfall 161* and *Rambling Jack*. *Like This?* will be published later this year.

Elizabeth Nannestad

Born in 1956, she currently lives in Auckland. She practises as a doctor. Her first book, *Jump*, was published in 1987.

Susan Allpress

Born 1957 in Auckland, she now lives in Northcote, Auckland. She taught in Auckland Central Intermediate School, and in 1987 attended Auckland University studying the Diploma in Drama. Her poems have been published in *Landfall, Rambling Jack,* and *Titirangi Poets,* and she was inlcuded in *The Globe Tapes* anthology.

Janet Potiki

Born in 1958, and now living at the beach in Paekakariki with her children. She is a multi-media artist working in theatre and dance drama, and she makes cloaks. She has published poetry in *Landfall* and *New Poets* and has written short stories.

Chérie Barford

Born 1960 in Auckland and now lives in Te Atatu North, Auckland. She is a relief-teacher at Avondale College. Her publications include poems in *Landfall, Ariel,* and a collection, *A Plea to the Spanish Lady,* 1985.

Jenny Bornholdt

Born 1960 in Lower Hutt and lives in Wellington. She currently works for Radio New Zealand and has publications in *Islands* and *Rambling Jack.* Her first book of poems *This Big Face* was published in April this year.

Kim Eggleston

Born 1960 in Picton, she now lives in Greymouth. She has published three collections of poetry: *From the Face to the Bin* 1984; *25 Poems* 1985 and, with others, *The Whole Crack* 1987.

Acknowledgements

For permission to reproduce copyright poems, grateful acknowledgement is made to the following publishers and copyright holders: Susan Allpress; Chérie Barford, Hard Echo Press for *A Plea to the Spanish Lady* 1985; Jenny Bornholdt, Victoria University Press for *This Big Face* 1988; Meg Campbell; Janet Charman, New Women's Press Ltd. for *Two Deaths in One Night* 1987; Christina Conrad; Ruth Dallas, University of Otago Press for *Collected Poems* 1987; Lauris Edmond, Oxford University Press for *Selected Poems* 1984 and *Seasons and Creatures* 1986; Kim Eggleston; Riemke Ensing; Fiona Farrell Poole, Auckland University Press for *Cutting Out* 1987; Anne French, Auckland University Press for *All Cretans are Liars* 1987 and *The Male as Evader* 1988; Sue Harlen, Mallinson Rendel for *Hook Hours* 1985; Dinah Hawken, Victoria University Press for *It Has No Sound and is Blue* 1987; Keri Hulme, Auckland University Press for *Moeraki Conversations* 1983; Helen Jacobs, Blackberry Press for *This Cording This Artery* 1984; Vivienne Joseph, John McIndoe Publishers for *A Desirable Property* 1984; Jan Kemp; Fiona Kidman, Richards Literary Agency, Heinemann for *Going to the Chathams* 1985; Michele Leggott; Judith Lonie, Iain Lonie; Rachel McAlpine, Mallinson Rendel for *Selected Poems* 1988; Heather McPherson; Cilla McQueen, John McIndoe Publishers for *Homing In* 1982, *Anti-Gravity* 1984, *Wild Sweets* 1986; Elizabeth Nannestad, Auckland University Press for *Jump* 1987; Joanna Paul; Janet Potiki; Elizabeth Smither, Auckland University Press for *Shakespeare Virgins* 1983, *The Legend of Marcello Mastroianni's Wife* 1981, and *Professor Musgrove's Canary* 1986, and Oxford University Press for *Casanova's Ankle* 1981.

Grateful acknowledgement is also made to the following publishers and editors of the publications listed below, who first published many of these poems: *And, Ariel, Broadsheet,* Caveman Press, Cicada Press, Coal-Black Press, *Craccum,* Hampson Hunt, Hawk Press, Home Print, Griffin Press, *Islands, Kiwi, Landfall, Morepork,* Nutshell Books, *NZ Listener, Parallax,* Prometheus Press, *Rambling Jack,* Spiral Collective, Strong John Press, Te Kotare Press, *The Globe Tapes, Titirangi Poets,* Tauranga Moana Press, University of Otago Bibliography Room, *Untold.*

Introduction

In 1977 *Private Gardens*, an anthology of New Zealand women poets, was published. The manner in which it was offered to the world was defensive. Bill Manhire, writing a review in *Islands*, said that there was a 'sense of protective worry about the whole book'.[1]

The editor of *Private Gardens*, Riemke Ensing, dealt with the difficulties she expected to arise out of the publication of a book devoted to poetry by women denying that any particular significance attaches to gender.

> A collection of women poets seems to me to be no more arbitrary than a collection of say, *Young* New Zealand poets, or *Recent* New Zealand poets . . . as arbitrary in fact as *any* collection whose tastes and slant must inevitably represent the editor's choice and point of view. Basically any anthology is no more than a collection of poems from a particular area or period or group of people, and as such is simply a classification of convenience.[2]

I do not think anyone writing now of an anthology of women poets would introduce it as a classification of convenience. However, a consciously constructed collection of poetry by women still raises political questions about the importance of gender in writing and publishing. It can be no accident that the reappearance of feminism in the sixties was succeeded by a huge increase in published women writers in the seventies and eighties. This fact alone raises questions about the way women have been evaluated in the literary history of New Zealand.

In his review of the *Penguin Book of New Zealand Verse*, edited by Ian Wedde and Harvey McQueen, C. K. Stead remarked, 'Since it's as well sometimes to spell things out laboriously let me say that I don't believe that during my lifetime any male editor in New Zealand, either of a literary periodical or an anthology, has ever discriminated against a woman writer on the grounds of sex.'[3] Stead's implication is that male writers were simply better

---

[1] Bill Manhire, 'Events as People: Notes on Private Gardens' *Islands* 19 p. 49.

[2] Riemke Ensing, 'Introduction' to *Private Gardens* p. 10.

[3] C. K. Stead, 'Two Views of the Penguin Book of New Zealand Verse' *Landfall* 155 p. 291.

than women, but if Dennis Glover's 'The Arraignment of Paris' or A.R.D. Fairburn's 'The Woman Problem' are taken as positioning an influential generation of male writers, then it is hard to see that women writers, perhaps especially poets, have not been disadvantaged. The domination of New Zealand literature by male writers over much of its history may in itself have acted as a condition against which only some women were prepared to struggle. Anne Else suggests something of the sort in her recent article for *Landfall* on the treatment of women poets in *Landfall* from 1947 to 1961:

> Women poets have always been part of a 'culture of exclusion'; but in post-war New Zealand (as in the West generally), as a pervasive, pseudo-scientific ideology of extreme masculine/ feminine differentiation grew and flourished, they had increasing difficulty in making their voice heard, let alone understood . . . it is not surprising that in the climate of the time, the prestigious critical response to their work in *Landfall* consisted at best of circumscribed, half-comprehending praise, and at worst of energetic misogynist attack. The surprising thing is that even a few women persisted . . .'[4]

Following the growth of feminism in New Zealand in the last two decades, there has been a dramatic increase in the number of women editors, publishers, and published women poets. The connection is obvious. Even so, a collection of women poets is still partly an attempt to equalize the publication ratios. In the fifties and sixties it was not uncommon to find whole years of *Landfall* without a single women poet. In recent large authoritative anthologies of New Zealand poetry the largest slice women have been given is one third, and in no case is a woman poet given ual weighting to the 'major' men. For some years feminist critics have been pointing to the way the 'feminine takes its place with the absence, silence or incoherence that discourse represses'.[5] It cannot be said any longer that the position of woman writers in New Zealand is that of absence or silence. But one of the

4 Anne Else, 'Not more than Man or Less; The Treatment of Women Poets in *Landfall* 1947-1961' *Landfall* 156 p. 443.
5 Mary Jacobus, 'The Difference of View' in *Feminist Literary Theory* ed. Mary Eagleton p. 217.

intentions of a collection like this one is to indicate the volume of writing by women that is not represented in anthologies, and to suggest that this constitutes a context at least as influential for women writers as the notion of collective nationality, and no more problematic. For this anthology of women poets, *Private Gardens* is an antecedent. What has changed between the two collections reflects their different positions in relation to feminism. *Private Gardens* was a pioneering idea with a number of poets who were largely unaffected by feminism: an anthology of women poets now is far from being a new idea, but its contributors constitute a new generation.

In her introduction, Ensing makes some generalizations about the work in *Private Gardens*:

> It is, I think, true to say that there is still a lot of 'politeness' in much of the work by women. There is a tendency towards the inoffensive, the safe, the pleasant and clean. Sexuality for instance is a subject treated with great care and only some seem able to go beyond that polite role usually associated with women . . . the New Zealand woman poet is still the 'Angel of the House' and the strident voice is largely absent. So too is experimentation with language.[6]

Karl Mutch, interviewing Ensing in *Landfall*, remarked, 'Probably the most general criticism which was levelled was the lack of range in the poetry . . . Some said that the poetry was not domestic but exhibited a lack of range — of emotional range.'[7] Bill Manhire said:

> 'There is a strangely cerebral atmosphere in *Private Gardens* . . . The imagination is hardly missing . . . but it is only there to make the poems poetic, it is not all owed to make the poems.'[8]

Making the poems poetic, lack of range — what these remarks begin to sound like are ways of talking about repression; poets who are writing within a notion of what poetry should be, what it should concern itself with, what is or is not poetic. The general

---

[6] Riemke Ensing, 'Introduction' to *Private Gardens* p. 12.

[7] Karl Mutch, 'Scarified with an Oyster Shell' *Landfall* 130 p. 152.

[8] Bill Manhire, op. cit. p. 49.

critical reaction to *Private Gardens* was to see in it work that is
'personal', limited, lacking 'range'.

The design of *Private Gardens*, with the poems interrupted by
mood-setting photographs or portraits of the poets, signals that
the poetry needs amplification in some way, that its qualities
require supplementary visual language; the poems are not 'serious'
enough to be read only in the medium in which they were written.
Even the title suggests a characterization of the work that is limited
by understood boundaries.

Images of reduction, separation, and blockage abound in *Private
Gardens*. Perhaps the point of writing for many women in *Private
Gardens* is, as Patricia Godsiff put it in her poem 'Hope', 'our dreams
will drown despair'. But it is a self-regarding despair, and there
is a predictability in much of the imagery used to describe it.
It is an unadventurous poetic. There is little anger in *Private Gardens*;
instead many women are cast upon the shores of their grief. Yet
at the level of imagery many of the poets are aware of a problematic
identity:

I hold my latter grief up to the light
And plural on a singular day I see
My redolent identity.

Tolla Williment, 'Tide at Flood'

Of course there are poets amongst the thirty-five in *Private
Gardens* who give the lie to these observations. Mary Stanley, Lauris
Edmond, Rachel McAlpine, Riemke Ensing, Elizabeth Smither are
all poets whose strengths were apparent or emerging in *Private
Gardens*, and there is a sense in which the presence and continuation
of these poets now makes the book seem a cobbling together
of two groups; some poets from whom little more has been heard,
and the established core of this collection. In retrospect, *Private
Gardens* is a book across a boundary, the historical boundary of
feminism.

One of the strongest expressions of feminism has been to
establish the literary history of women. In an interview with Harry
Ricketts, Rachel McAlpine has said:

It's actually getting published that makes people into poets I
reckon. Because then you've got an incentive, you've got this

whole web of expectation that you'll go on writing . . . that you're going to get better, and you do! Whereas if you're writing away in private and showing two friends, it never develops.[9]

In some important respects feminism has been about the move from private to public; from writing poems and stowing them in the cupboard, as Lauris Edmond has described her young life, to publication and professionalism. Associated with this move is an observable change in the way women writers see the function of poetry: a move from the celebration of feeling to an investigation of what it is to be a woman poet; a reconsideration of role and stereotype; an exploration of the various kinds of activity poetry can engage in. As editor I have selected poets and poems to emphasize this change.

A major concern in this anthology is to give a sense of the literary history of women by showing the body of work, outside that of the established, well-known poets, which is less accessible to the general reader. As a general principle I have included as many poets as possible while still allowing each a reasonable quota of poems. The selection is not intended to be read hierarchically: although some poets do have a larger number of poems, this reflects the comparative bulk of their published work and is not intended as a judgement that they are worth more. There are also a number of poets who have not yet published a collection. Editorially I have tried to suggest the energy, expansion, and difference shown by New Zealand women poets in recent years. The observable lack is in writing by Māori women. As a non-Māori speaker I have included only poems written wholly or mostly in English. Consequently this anthology does not represent the full range of Māori women poets. Without their work the full dimensions of the literary history of women in this country cannot be realized, and a unilingual anthology is only a partial representation of it.

Research for this collection revealed a surge in publication by women in 1974-1975, which has since increased. I decided to maximize this surge by limiting the historical range of the work I researched to 1965-1987. In fact this has meant by far the greatest concentration of work comes from the last ten years, when a

[9] Rachel McAlpine, *Talking About Ourselves* ed. Harry Ricketts p. 32.

number of women became established poets in the mainstream of New Zealand writing, and many new poets appeared. In their work there are obvious ways in which the feminism has undermined and challenged the kinds of generalizations Ensing was able to make.

Most obviously, and perhaps least interestingly, the politeness that Ensing saw as a feature of work by women, the unwillingness to tackle anything not pleasant and clean, has disappeared. Menstruation, sex, particularly featuring women as active lovers, pregnancy, rape, and incest are frequent subjects; anger and hostility are expressed in the work of most women and often characterize the work of feminists. This openness extends to the use of a deliberately impolite vocabulary and an interest in physicality; the notion that poetry includes some sensations and not others has been abandoned.

> Well it's been a good day for me,
> A little job done, a big one started;
> torso buzzing, knees vibrating
> and waves of semen oozing
> on their expedition south.
>
> Rachel McAlpine, 'A Good Day'

However, these in a sense are surface changes, though they indicate how the boundaries of woman as poet have shifted and enlarged.

There seem to me to be two main differences between *Private Gardens* and this collection. The first is the way in which poets in this collection are interested in exploring forms of identity. The sense of many selves is common to much of the poetry here and is expressed both in an interest in the way women signal themselves to others and in explorations of gender. Much of the poetry uses imagery of encoding familiar to women — clothes, houses, names — or satirizes conventional notions of women as happy consumers, efficient housewives, or passive lovers. Cilla McQueen's poems 'Silly thing' and 'Timepiece' make fun of consumerism and housework, and Rachel McAlpine's 'bird-woman' is woman as devouring lover and, powerful animal. Lovers,

mothers, and daughters — these are constant subjects in this
anthology; investigated, criticized, and imaged.

> i am thinking of the ram on my mothers vegetable dish
> the ram was glued to the side
> a single fanatic's eye looking out
> the dish loomed white and terrible
> i always watched the ram
> i seed past the ram
> all the while the dish stayed white and unchanging
> my mother rising above it
> a caged bird
>
> *Christina Beer, 'This Fig Tree Has Thorns'*

In re-examining gender relationships women are questioning
received identities, which is sometimes a celebration, as well as
a rejection or a restructuring. It is in relationships with men that
there is most unease expressed and I think there is a general
sense in this collection that the lives of women emerge in all
their strong narrative detail quite independently from the men
who might be connected with them.

> If mama is the word
> babies make
> with mouth and breast
> it's father that's abstract
> pure invention —
> handy I suppose for opening
> and closing doors
> yet you can do it
> with less fuss without
>
> *Anne French, 'Abstraction' from 'Photographs for Daddy'*

Love poems form a not inconsiderable part of the way women
identify themselves in these poems, but the tone is determinedly
unsentimental: it is a discerning and unforgiving eye on the whole,
which shows the shapes of gender.

> The subject of children and wives
> was thoroughly aired ('I get plenty of high class sex
> at home', he murmured, 'it's our minds which will enrich
> this entire situation,' and then

proceeded to demolish the myth
of minds in the feminine gender.)

Fiona Kidman, 'A Businessman's Lunch'

The other main difference that struck me in comparing the shifts of ten years is that the fictiveness of language, the business of being a poet, is a subject that recurs throughout the collection. Whereas in *Private Gardens* there was little engagement with what the poets were doing as poets, there are many poets in this collection who are concerned with the nature of language, its constructions and deconstructions, the world of fictiveness on the page. With the exploration of the boundaries of language and meaning comes poetry that is sharp and conscious:

There are so many things
the poem can't do.
Where for example in this note
book scribble and drawing
these cryptic messages for later
is the smell of salt & sea
weed & the wind & the dry
grass waving up from the hills?

Riemke Ensing, 'Paikea Bay' from 'Track With Tide Coming In'

In *Private Gardens* there is no sense that the world of the poem is not closed and sufficient. In this collection many poems speak partially and consciously of fictions and of the fictions they are; of how language speaks the poet and her continuations, of lives to lives, of language and the world, of poem to reader.

All roads lead to other roads.
Every arrival a departure.
We swoop to the centre. Drive through the frame . . .

Strange how loudly paint
can whoop and yell.
How it can hiss and slide.

Fiona Farrell Poole, 'Charts to Shores Rarely Visited'

A number of poets use language to suggest other media, especially paint: the detailed visual surface of Cilla McQueen's 'Vegetable Garden Poem II', or the insistence on colour in Joanna Paul's poetry; there is in general a preoccupation with the kinds of seeing and the kinds of making possible in art empowered by language.

> Time and again
> time and again I tried to write a goddess song.
> Now that I have fleshed the lyric tongue a poem
> stirs. It breaks from its inhabitants. Red shapes
> blaze in the patchwork quilt. Here are two women
> naked on a bed.
>
> *Heather McPherson, 'Theology and a Patchwork Absolute'*

In the work of some younger and more recent poets, Susan Allpress, Jenny Bornholdt, Michelle Leggott, the interest in making, in fabrication, is expressed in fluid open forms. The work of Michelle Leggott, for instance, exploits and shifts the gaps between text and reader:

> don't explain
> your peculiar charm
> (that quick view)
> against the downroad
>
> each working morning
>
> move across
> to the other window
>
> to be shown
>
> *Michelle Leggott, 'Yellow Pencil'*

Different forms, different subjects: reserve and prettiness are less characteristic of poetry currently written by women than is the description of menstruation, pregnancy, or sex. Maybe a new orthodoxy is setting in, although there are many directions opening out in the poetry of women and a great many more ways to read the work in this collection than I have suggested here. What dominates for me is the sense of a female voice that wants to work out how it really is in the later years of the twentieth century. In the work of Dinah Hawken, for example, words have power, as artefacts and fictions, and as part of the serious discrimination of value. Hawken's poetry is about the dominating anxieties of the late twentieth century and how to maintain humanity amongst them: in her poem, 'Balance', Hawken speaks to and for women from the exploded heart of the battlefield. It is a question that most of us ask.

> So I take hold of this poem
> which has come from the front.
> From the newspaper. From a narrow crack
> in a stack of exploded concrete.
> From the hand of a paratrooper, reaching out
> through the crack to a friend, in Lebanon.
> From the voice of a marine, pleading
> under collapsed stories of man-made rock,
> 'Don't leave me here.' And what I ask
> from far below my own life,
> as the rescue work goes on, and what
> we must know in this time of crisis, yes,
> and grief, hunching towards the best,
> most ambitious dead end of all, is where
> are the women, where exactly are we?
>
> *Dinah Hawken, 'Balance'*

Ruth Dallas

In Central Otago

Seek foliage and find
Among cracked boulders
Scab of lichen, thyme.

Seek a burgeoning tree
Discover
Upended witches' brooms.

Seek grass and tread
Stiff sheet of ice drawn
Over the land dead.

Moon country.
No one could live here,
In the houses squat on shingle.

Fields scorched,
Snow gripping the mountains;
Nothing could recover

From such desolation,
Jack Frost's sheep-run,
Mirror of the bleak mind.

But come back in a month —
See blanketing the slits
And sockets of the land's skeleton

Square eiderdowns of peach-bloom,
Old crone, Plum, unpick
A feather mattress from a bald stone.

A New Dress

I don't want a new dress, I said.
My mother plucked from her mouth ninetynine pins.
I suppose there are plenty, she said, *girls of ten*
Who would be glad to have a new dress.

Snip-snip. Snip-snip. The cold scissors
Ate quickly as my white rabbit round my arm.

She won't speak to me if I have a new dress!
My feet rattled on the kitchen floor.

How can I fit you if you won't stand still?

My tears made a map of Australia
On the sofa cushion; from the hot centre
My friend's eyes flashed, fierce as embers.
She would not speak to me, perhaps never again.
She would paralyse me with one piercing look.

I'd rather have my friend than a new dress!

My mother wouldn't understand, my grownup mother
Whose grasshopper thimble winked at the sun,
And whose laughter was made by small waves
Re-arranging seashells on Australia's shore.

Iceland Poppies

You ask me
  What I am saying
    In my poems.
What am I saying?
  That everything
    Is falling from us,
  We, too, are falling;

And so this day, this
  Hour, with the sun shining
    In its customary fashion

And the wind blowing the trees,
You and I,
Sitting behind windows
Discussing poems,
This moment, every moment, falls,
Is falling.

More precious
Than any fiery diamond
Is the flowering human heart,
Opening like a poppyhead
And like a poppy falling.

Kyeburn Diggings

Someone has been looking under the stones
For gold,
Has lifted every stone and knocked it clean,
Brown mountain stones,
White river stones,
A stock of cannon balls
Pitched into hills for the frost to crack,
Sun to bake,
Deck for the lizard to roast his back.
Whether gold was found or no,
The stones are scrubbed sterile as snow,
Too hot, too cold for grass to grow.

The desert thorn now tries her skill,
To shift or anchor at her will.

Living with a Cabbage-Tree

A cabbage-palm is not an interesting tree.
Its single trunk resembles a telegraph-pole.
Botanists say it is not a tree at all,
But a lily, grown exceptionally rampant.
This, I think, could happen only in New Zealand,
Where birds have left us skeletons as big as horses'.

I did not want a cabbage-tree in the garden.
There's plenty of room on the Canterbury plains
Where a tree of any kind relieves the eye.
Its life began as a little harmless flax-bush,
I thought a pot-plant — ornamental leaves
Someone had planted out for variety of foliage.
I had hardly turned my back when it soared up
Into a shape like a coconut-palm in a strait-jacket.

The flax-bush-part is elevated now, say fifteen feet,
And casts the smallest patch of shadow and the fastest
In the garden. It's enough to cover your head;
But if you take a chair outside you must be prepared
To shift from west to east more quickly
Than you have ever chased the shelter of a tree.

I like the way the shadow of its bole
Moves like the finger of a giant sun-dial
Over the concrete; that's rather romantic;
Reminding us that time is passing, passing;
And cats declare it without peer for sharpening claws.
But it's a dull tree, inclined to fancy itself
As a musical instrument, when the wind blows,
Sometimes tuning up like an orchestra.
You listen expectantly. But nothing happens.
The wind drops and it falls silent.

In the University Library

I am swallowed by a whale
Whose ribs are well furnished
With writing material, books,
A choice of coffee or tea.

From portholes I observe
Clouds disperse
Or gather in threatening storm.
Seabirds pass overhead

Emitting their coarse laughter.
I am walled behind glass

Where snow does not fall
Nor gales blow. I write poems,

Frame incantations
Against being digested by the whale.

Black on White

I pulled the fish-hook of my grief
And projected it on the wall
In a stark painting; Indian ink
On a stretch of white paper,

Silhouette of a ripped thorntree,
Broken-backed on the horizon,
Black lightning forking the sky;
But still I felt a thorn.

I pulled, and cried, *All done!*
Then found another thorn.
And when that thorn was pulled

Splinters of bone worked through the flesh,
Even after the skin was healed.
Grief is pulling all my bones.

Photographs of Pioneer Women

You can see from their faces
Life was not funny,
The streets, when there were streets,
Tugging at axles,
The settlement ramshackle as a stack of cards.
And where there were no streets, and no houses,
Save their own roof of calico or thatch,
The cows coming morning and afternoon
From the end-of-world swamp,
Udders cemented with mud.

There is nothing to equal pioneering labour
For wrenching a woman out of shape,
Like an old willow, uprooted, thickening.
See their strong arms, their shoulders broadened
By the rhythmical swing of the axe, or humped
Under loads they donkeyed on their backs.
Some of them found time to be photographed,
With bearded husband, and twelve or thirteen children,
Looking shocked, but relentless,
After first starching the frills in their caps.

Pioneer Woman with Ferrets

Preserved in film,
As under glass,
Her waist nipped in,
Skirt and sleeves
To ankle, wrist,
Voluminous
In the wind,
Hat to protect
Her Victorian complexion,
Large in the tussock
She looms,
Startling as a moa.
Unfocussed,
Her children
Fasten wire-netting
Round close-set warrens,
And savage grasses
That bristle in a beard
From the rabbit-bitten hills.
She is monumental
In the treeless landscape.
Nonchalantly she swings
In her left hand
A rabbit,
Bloodynose down,
In her right hand a club.

Lauris Edmond

The Third Person

I do not know how to describe the third person but
on days when the doves came hurtling over the city
flung upwards in great purring armfuls outside your window
and fell, piling like black hail on ledges of buildings
across the street, he came in, he was there — let us
call him a man. He preened his purple feathers.

His eyes were brilliant, unblinking; he became
servant, interpreter, master and miracle-maker,
intricate designer of harmony out of
our broken fragments of love and confusion; I thought
you had summoned him for me, understanding
my weakness. I found him beautiful.

I came to you one cold evening in April,
the summer doves had flown, you were busy;
in the hard blue light the third person was very tall
and sharpened his steely claws meticulously.
When I showed my fear you moved slowly to stand beside him
and stared at me calmly without recognition.

Eden Cultivated

Think of her coming in from the garden,
her hair blowing and the green breath
of summer drifting across the verandah
— the long grass, and the smell of apples —
behind her a blazing February sky,
the first thistledowns, and the haze;
see her drag out the old capacious
preserving pan from the darkened pantry
smelling of spices and orange peel,
and notice the small lines round her eyes,
the bones of her bending shoulders . . .
and wait — for how do you know, this time,
if she will offer you one apple
or many, or possibly none at all?

All Possession is Theft

There had been rain in the morning and a chaffinch,
before we surprised it, strutted beside a pool
on the lawn; the house was white, polite, had nothing
to say, but the trees — the great, well-heeled, patrician
trees — turned their green shoulders aside;
the pohutukawa has lineage, I would be certain
to make faux pas across its genealogies.
And my foot slipped between clay and concrete,
a magpie jeered and left, noisily.
The land agent drooled his obsequies — the previous
occupant, psychiatrist . . . I thought I saw him
at the window frowning over his sad case histories,
neglecting his paths but cared for by his trees;
and touched one, tentatively, found instead
its green shawl of long three-fingered leaves,
a pink flower luxurious as an orchid, and in
the shadow a single fruit, narrow, golden,
the poised and secret guardian of an old season's
accumulations. 'Banana passion fruit'
— the agent, natural for a moment, pressed on
'The elevation here . . .' I turned aside
breathless, feeling faintly lecherous, closed
my hand about that small old bag of gold
and, with a quick tug, took it. I live here now.

A Difficult Adjustment

It takes time, and there are setbacks;
on Monday, now, you were all ennui
and malice; but this morning I am
pleased with my handiwork: your
stick figure moves, your two eyes
are large and dark enough, your
expression is conveniently mild.
You have begun to disagree with me,
but weakly, so that I can easily prove
you wrong. In fact you are entirely
satisfactory.

I suppose, really, you are
dead. But someone silently lies down
with me at night and shows a soothing
tenderness. I have killed the pain
of bone and flesh; I suffer no laughter
now, nor hear the sound of troubled
voices speaking in the dark.

The Names

Six o'clock, the morning still and
the moon up, cool profile of the night;
time small and flat as an envelope —
see, you slip out easily: do I know you?
Your names have still their old power,
they sing softly like voices across water.

Virginia Frances Martin Rachel Stephanie
Katherine — the sounds blend and chant
in some closed chamber of the ear, poised
in the early air before echoes formed.
Suddenly a door flies open, the music
breaks into a roar, it is everywhere;

now it's laughter and screaming, the crack
of a branch in the plum tree, the gasping
and blood on the ground; it is sea-surge
and summer, 'Watch me!' sucked under
the breakers; the hum of the lupins, through
sleepy popping of pods the saying of names.

And all the time the wind that creaked in
the black macrocarpas and whined in the wires
was waiting to sweep us away; my children who
were my blood and breathing I do not know you:
we are friends, we write often, there are
occasions, news from abroad. One of you is dead.

I do not listen fearfully for you in the night,
exasperating you with my concern,
I scarcely call this old habit love —
yet you have come to me this white morning,
and remind me that to name a child is brave,
or foolhardy; even now it shakes me.

The small opaque moon, wafer of light,
grows fainter and disappears; but
the names will never leave me, I hear
them calling like boatmen far over
the harbour at first light. They will sound
in the dreams of your children's children.

Epiphany

for Bruce Mason

I saw a woman singing in a car
opening her mouth as wide as the sky,
cigarette burning down in her hand
— even the lights didn't interrupt her
though that's how I know the car
was dignified — cream and sleek;
it is harder for a rich woman . . .

Of course the world went on
fucking itself up just the same —
and I hate the idea of stabbing at
poems as though they are flatfish,
but how can you ignore a perfect lyric
in a navy blue blouse, carolling away
as if it's got two minutes out of
the whole of eternity, just
to the corner of Wakefield Street —

which after all is a very long life
for any ecstasy to be given.

Catching it

I saw three men looking
towards the sea:
they were on a seat, laughing —
three small brown foxy Frenchmen,
and the funniness of it
licking them over
like forked lightning.

In all of the ticking of time
it can never have happened before,

not like this, not exactly —
and the one by the sea wall
had a slack old jacket
done up with frogs
and a black fingernail
and a hole in the knee of his pants
— just to make sure.

Going to Moscow

The raspberries they gave us for dessert
were delicious, sharp-tasting and furry,
served in tiny white bowls; you spooned cream
on to mine explaining I'd find it sour.
The waitress with huge eyes and a tuft
of hair pinched like a kewpie so wanted
to please us she dropped two plates as
she swooped through the kitchen door.
No one could reassure her. Snow was falling;
when you spoke, across the narrow white
cloth I could scarcely hear for the distance
nor see you through floating drifts.

Then the tall aunt brought out her dog,
a small prickly sprig like a toy; we put on
our coats and in the doomed silence Chekhov
the old master nodded at us from the wings.

At the last my frozen lips would not
kiss you, I could do nothing but talk
to the terrible little dog: but you
stood still, your polished shoes swelling up
like farm boots. There are always some
who must stay in the country when others
are going to Moscow. Your eyes were
a dark lake bruised by the winter trees.

Word

'It is perfect' you say
and my pain listens
wearing its evil grin:
I grow faint
it leans over me
monitoring my defeat.
Wind cries at the corners
of winter streets.

'. . . because complete' you go on
with gentleness. I draw in,
flesh achieves
a new density.
I am a hurt cell
dark with life
that somewhere else
will elbow into joy.

Signs

The pronoun is
a tiny instrument we use
to unpick our lives; so 'I'
and 'you' begin to show
beneath the old shared knots
of 'us', so 'ours' is spoilt for 'mine'.
We do not know the dreadful pleasure

of our industry until
the rag's too weak to take
the weight of joy or compromise,
the pull and tear of love.

The Killing

Oh love's persistent,
won't give up its hold;
dismissed, creeps back
to tap all night at
sleeping windows; silenced,
maunders on — laughs too,
even here in the stained
dust to show how this
poor hen, grotesquely
on its feet, running as
it bleeds, still pursues
that old life of dirt
and sunshine our tomahawk
has shortly said is gone.

Latter Day Lysistrata

It is late in the day of the world
and the evening paper tells of developed
ways of dying; five years ago we would not
have believed it. Now I sit on the grass
in fading afternoon light crumpling pages
and guessing at limits of shock, the point
of repudiation; my woman's mind, taught
to sustain, to support, staggers at this
vast reversal. I can think only of
the little plump finches that come
trustingly into the garden, moving
to mysterious rhythms of seeds and
seasons; I have no way to conceive
the dark maelstrom where men may spin
in savage currents of power — is it
power? — and turn to stone, to steel,

no longer able to hear such small throats'
hopeful chirping nor see these tiny
domestic posturings, the pert shivering
of feathers. They know only the fire
in the mind that carries them down
and down in a wild and wrathful wind.

I do not know how else
the dream of any man on earth can be
'destroy all life, leaving
buildings whole . . .'

Let us weep for these men, for
ourselves, let us cry out as they bend
over their illustrious equations; let us
tell them the cruel truth of bodies,
skin's velvet bloom, the scarlet of
bleeding. Let us show them the vulnerable
earth, the transparent light that slips
through slender birches falling over
small birds that sense in the miniscule
threads of their veins the pulses of
every creature — let these men breathe
the green fragrance of the leaves, here
in this gentle darkness let them convince me,
here explain their preposterous imaginings.

The outside room

It was the moon poised with a bright patience
low over the paddocks, the silence standing
about in surprise as though newly arrived,
the constant soft bleat of the sheep
and the earth, most of all the earth itself

sending up its unaccountably tender emanations
and winy smell, telling me what dew can do
to sap-heavy grass and sheep shit, and
to the sheep too, obscurely coiled
in the oil emollients of their wool —

all this, as I crept out in the no-time
after midnight, going to pee by the fence
squatting in the cool heady freshness, night's
elbow flung over the hill and the strange
spare light of the stars beyond —

all whispering, explaining, declaring
that the persecuted earth has not yet
resigned its ancient romance with seaons
and creatures; and so clearly my body
couldn't help exulting as it tiptoed back

over the cold crush of the grass, stones
by the door, and I saw without looking the dark window
behind which the young lay asleep together
holding once again safe until morning
their dream of a lifetime to come.

Tempo

In the first month I think
it's a drop in a spider web's
necklace of dew

at the second a hazel-nut; after,
a slim Black-eyed Susan demurely folded
asleep on a cloudy day

then a bush-baby silent as sap
in a jacaranda tree, but blinking
with mischief

at five months it's an almost-caught
flounder flapping back
to the glorious water

six, it's a song
with a chorus of basses: seven, five grapefruit
in a mesh bag that bounces on the hip
on a hot morning down at the shops

a water-melon next — green oval
of pink flesh and black seeds, ripe
waiting to be split by the knife

nine months it goes faster, it's a bicycle
pedalling for life over paddocks
of sun
no, a money-box filled with silver half-crowns
a sunflower following the clock
with its wide-open grin
a storm in the mountains, spinning rocks
down to the beech trees
three hundred feet below
— old outrageous Queen Bess's best dress
starched ruff and opulent tent of a skirt
packed with ruffles and lace
no no, I've remembered, it's a map
of intricate distinctions
purples for high ground burnt umber
for foothills green for the plains
and the staggering blue
of the ocean beyond
waiting and waiting and
aching
with waiting

no more alternatives! Suddenly now
you can see my small bag of eternity
pattern of power
my ace my adventure
my sweet-smelling atom
my planet, my grain of miraculous dust
my green leaf, my feather
my lily my lark
look at her, angels —
this is my daughter.

The capable spirit

Oh yes happiness arrives all right,
it set itself up here last Friday
adopting like Maui all necessary forms
to suit the present adventure

chattering in the weatherboards
of a lean-to kitchen, rustling like paper
in tacked bright prints on the walls
gloating over our shoulders
at these complete little feet
faint-stroked eyebrows
half-cat's-eye pale shell fingernails
unfocused blue eyes;

try animal, mineral, vegetable, this is
the most various magic any of us will know;
in a bedscape of milky breast
it moons and whispers, goes to perch
on a yellow bucket in the bathroom

rash phantom pretending to command
all the great ceremonies in this one;
and it does seem just now, in this flimsy cottage,
it can do anything. Clever with love,
it is busy composing a life.

Hymns Ancient and Modern

On a rough night spinning past
the macrocarpas' violent shadows
wind wrenched the car sideways
till for very apprehension I began singing
the purposeful hymns of childhood
All Hail the Power   O Worship the King
Su-un of my So-oul Thou Sa-aviour Dear

mist sent its wraiths whirling
queerly over the farms as I intoned
Rock of Ages, even at last Lest We Forget
(oh the smell of chrysanthemums
on terrible Anzac Days!).

But truly on Tinakori Hill
the dark spurs motioned me past
and I came on home. Up steps to the windy door
key in the lock   the first light switch
mail in a pile on the table
your letter.

'It happened last week, in England.
The children have been told.'
Six-year-old Josie, died of a brain tumour.
A small child, pretty, inclined to giggle
— that's really all I know.
How silent the wind is
it has no voice now
no song. It is just wind, after all
just air
the cruel and stupid air that will always
come and go at random —

in All Saints Sunday School
at a death we sang Abide With Me
in our effortless thin voices
and looked out the window
savouring all the Sunday dinners
still to come.

The process

In a time of desolation
to recall the rich acres of summer
is to know you are alone; the others
have gone, or changed irrecoverably —

it is as though change itself
is the auctioneer who put under the hammer
a precious expanse, knocking it down
to the bead-bright eyes of loss, illness
separation, death —

so we no longer lean on our elbows
at Frank's narrow table, his trout mornay
steaming under the lifted spoon
nor sprawl in the study
where poems burgeoned and broke
against Mexican embroideries,
Meg stumbling over our legs as she
ran out, weeping, and Vincent spoke
of white horses in a manic moonlight
somewhere in the Cotswolds — while all the time

outside lay love's precarious landscape
ours without act of possession
the place that, as we talked,
time had already noted yard by silent yard
and marked for sale by dissolution.

Dunedin in July

After fifty the mind's muscles begin to
slacken, the view it encompasses grows
broader, yet I think more lightly held.

This morning on a cold Otago hillside
I take in Mount Cargill, snow beard
untrimmed, the spires of sober churches,

the steely light of the sky, near me
in black earth under the ngaio tree
a single snowdrop two inches high;

and in the same moment, precisely set
in its narrower frame, the small hill sprinkled
with beech tree shadow in summer

a young woman walking and watching
beginning thirty years ago to learn
all I have inescapably become.

She is quiet and merry and spry, secure
in the power she has no idea
she will lose or relinquish repeatedly

in the anguish of later seasons —
she is so close I can almost touch her
nearly smile into those unseeing green eyes;

behind her the hills and the city
tilt and steady in the piercing southern light
as though to confer the outline

of one horizon on older and more confused,
more hurtful angles. Standing here
I can just smell the scent of that flower.

Helen Jacobs

Statement

It would seem easier to draw
a pencil line, cat curve
on cushioned chair,
the book, the arched fern
and violet on the table there,
which in itself would say —

words with difficulty
convey the point reached —

Start again with the curtains
and the chair and the rug,
a thirty year composition;
stitching the rug, the many folds
of curtain falling, deposition
fold along fold.

I am drawing an old arrangement
a still life accepted interior
exterior to our through walking,
calendar print over mind movement;
but will the pencil lines invisibly flow
invisibly query the cat on the chair?

Autumn Day in Sunshine

I hesitate to curl
the paper smoke
up
into the clear cut day,

or wisp a smear on the
purity a single spider
thread
crystal edges;

not to stir the ash
of the years, but to hold
unclouded
this allowance of clarity.

Letter from a Sister

You write of ordinary health
and the cold wind that has salt burnt
the shrubs again, and of children
running in and out as they do
perpetually in your house.

But it is the new small dog
fluffy, tail curled, and the bleak
sentences that our sister
is submerged again, wounded
in giving, that spin me back
into the centrifuge, to
the 'before' days, before we
broke off differently from
the centre.

You end your letter talking of
spinning wheels.

            And the thread goes back
and back to the pattern already
charted–a small alert black dog,
you spelling stories to younger ones.
Watching, watching
I see our sister generous and
in defiance, winding her offerings
into her own body bandage.

From being distant
I answer your letter immediately.

Poem

I cannot make your days, your nights,
other than grey replicas
                    of the sapped wood
but I can tell you
that the small hole
I put the seedling cineraria in
was black and wet and smelt of worm-soil
where soon the head of warm petals will glow;

and amongst the tangled green and dead
of the matting grass
                    in bush dark was
a slightness of purple
of the first violet;
and in the wind rush
that poured through me as I moved from stooping
a tug of our days that were creviced by small things —

            time cracks between the rock
            the jewel of colour —
            Can I not offer you small things?

Hello!

You rang six times
six times saying:

the storm has
beaten up the road —

they have carried the
tree trunks away off it —

and then

the power pole has been
saved from tottering —

the boat debris is dumped in
orange and white and blue shards
and patches raggle-taggle —

you rang to say
the wind and water are sailing
away together glissading up
through the rooftops —

you rang
you love your yellow storm gear
leaving your face to the wear of rain —

You
loving wild
calling six times.

Enclosure

Taking the cocoon of a car
cassettes selected
setting it all up
within a skin of yellow metal
and barrier glass we
seal into our own inside —
                              blood heat.

You drive expertly with one hand.

Sunsets are admitted
dove cloud
white pampas stiff hedged
in a low light
patchy cows —
the willows obscure themselves
totally.

I rub your fingernail
sliding into the pumpkin-
orange farmhouse lights

— chrysalis dreaming time,
the tentative star
moon icicle on wings

a thread

— *to butterfly*
I think it will be easy soon
to slip out of my skin —

You have already practised
making me into a photograph —

You are more at ease
without my voice —

I am seldom the flesh
at your side —

You can fill the rooms
with your isolation —

There. Five jerks
and I have metamorphosed
into an idea inside my own head.
I left the house tidy for you.

Judith Lonie

Three Berlin Postcards

IF SNOW
is a particular event
a picture postcard set
precisely
in a sultry Christmas
or even a real fall fleeting
as a warm winter,
here it falls like rain
insistently . . .
not far from the woodcutter's cottage
wolves leap in the Grunewald
and hunger and want are not difficult
to imagine

SPRING RECOILS
from her nakedness displayed
for sale on Kurfürstendamm
rising
out of the tulip stall,
the Porno film hoarding.
She dresses herself
modishly

GO EAST
and up their new T.V.
tower you can see the whole
(they are filling in the blanks)
divided city.
From this height texture
is irrelevant, the glossy postcard
is as true a picture.
Unter den Linden
it will rain soon.

The Lie

In cold waking I know
there is a lie in our life
somewhere: you want me
to state it, but I can't
lay my hand on it.   I only
know that somewhere I saw
a skullful of dried snakeheads.

Paradox

You so tender are so

rough, so coarse are so
delicate: if it were not so

you would not fit me.

Enter the Hero

Black sea swelling behind
blinding white light ahead
he is totally unprepared
but he must take action now
or never
He draws in a great painful gulp of air
as if his life depended upon it
It does

On Colin McCahon's Gate Series

You have to work hard here
if you want to be in the picture:

You stand in the dark
looking up

A
  S
    L
      A
        N
          T

to a SQUARE of light
but can't find the turning
at conventional left or right.

(The SQUARE becomes RHOM
                        BOID
disappears at the sun's turning.)
Now you stand in a light-filled desert
looking down at that black night
you cannot escape, nor the sun's burning.

Near the end of the journey
you strike point blank black

O
B
L
O
N
G and immediately enter a
RECTANGLE of pure light:

He did right
putting us in the picture.

Meg Campbell

Solitary confinement

Like a fisherman I wait
until the words are caught
on my line. My bait is silence.
Between me and the world
are locked doors, passages
and more locked doors.
There is no one else in this wing.

It was peaceful this morning at dawn
I was locked up with my thoughts
catching them on a hook
as they darted about. My anchor
settled in bright sand.

In the half-light I peered
at the words sprawled on the page.
A bird sang in the hospital garden
and outside the unbreakable
glass window the flowers grew
without supervision, and the sun
lifted into the sky of its own volition.

What dreams may come

Morning arrives with a shock
and the sleepers stir
in the long white ward
as the key turns in the lock.
My mouth drains dry of dreams.
Nurse stretches, lifts knitting
from a pool of light into her bag
all meaning speared on those needles.
She is leaving. Her ghostly charges
surround her asking for a light
for their morning cigarettes.
She calls them 'ladies'

with a touch or irony and sighs.
And the ghostly ladies sigh
and fidget down corridors
long as nun's prayers.
In the dining room, bewildered
at formica tables amongst teacup clatter,
they watch while bread-and-butter knives
are counted and handed out.
From the window I see
a high, dreaming hedge
between hospital grounds and cemetery.
A fallen jam-jar spills its dead
gladioli on a grave.

Hole in the head

I have sung every song I know this night —
my fourth in isolation. By morning
I am hoarse, and no one hears me
but the ladies who kick the door, "You're
down for Treatment and serves you right —
making a disturbance!" But now they come,
nurses who are warders who are nurses,
with hard, frightened hands. I plead
and fight and pull off my clothes in a corner.
Here is the doctor, nightmare eyes bulging,
master of the machine which glides to the bed
where I'm held, temples bared, teeth
clamped on a rubber gag. "How are you Mrs Jones?"
he says, just as the Magistrate did.
There is a smell of meths and then
no air — no time to breathe . . . I leave them
through a hole drilled by fire in my temples,
escaping the explosion that ends all worlds.

Long Day's Journey

I have tucked my needs away
under my skirt. I am
my mother's good daughter,
will work for you devotedly,
never asking for reward.

Teach us to serve Thee
as Thou deservest . . .

I think you an exacting man
pressing me
in my white exhaustion
to cook, clean, brew more tea,
to wear a nice face
and look to my tasks
with a good grace.

Teach us to toil
and not to seek for rest . . .

Under my skirt I have hidden
my unsuitable self.
A terrible prayer, learned
at a school for young ladies
shortcircuits my brain.

Teach us to labour
and not to ask for any reward . . .

Found Wanting

Mother, I try to understand you
by searching those long years
of childhood, when you'd straighten
my parting, and button me up
correctly, seeing something irritating
that you couldn't express.

And I'd ask, 'Am I pretty?'
sensing your reservations.
'You are . . . when you smile'
was the nearest you came to praise.
(I rarely smile when happy, being absorbed.)
Your words groomed me

like the fretful lick of a cat,
yet I remained 'untidy'.
Why did you fret? Since then
I have sometimes torn hair and skin
until pain formed a film
over your distracted eyes.

Maui

I have snapped off my burning
fingers, and given them to you
one by one, but you have thrown them
in the stream to amuse yourself.
I am fed up with you!
When next you come to me begging
for fire, I shall be ashes.
I hear that you intend to cheat
Death — a serious matter —
but, when I see you crushed
between her thighs, I shall laugh
until my fires rekindle,
and my tears steam, and spit.

This Morning at Dawn

Pirate! I woke this morning
to find you anchored in me.
You had come in through the Heads
at first light. My plump whiteness
amuses you vastly. Your teeth gleam
and your eyes are dark slits.
Shamelessly you have beached
your long-boat high on the sand . . .

You handsome bastard,
how is it that you are
so very sure of your ground?
The tide is going out, amigo —
take care that the water
doesn't drown you, leaving only
your cocked hat floating
on the surface . . . Is it true, then,
that pirates never learn to swim?

In the Fullness of Time

I came up through a dark tunnel
of trees late this evening,
heard the dogs bark
from the top of the hill.
The track rose steeply
and branches caught at my hair,
above me, a pattern of stars
below, the dark space of the sea.
I knew you'd not be there,
inside the house.
Later, I found in a drawer
a few of your old clothes
paint-stained and torn,
that I had wanted to burn
but you wouldn't let me . . .
I was certain, then,
that you meant to return.

Winter Letter

Tonight the air is cold
and the leaves of iceplant
are red on the cliff edge.
I have searched the garden
for signs of those small trees
planted before you left.
They are thrusting upwards,
small banners of triumph
telling me you were here
and will be here again . . .
I only half believe.

Across the Straits the sky
is orange beneath clouds;
indoors, an armchair holds
me comfortably . . . I'm, like
a fire banked up for the night.
I'm waiting for the sound
of your step on the path
and the excited dogs
leaping against you. When
you return, I'll show you
the iceplant on the cliff —
how it has reddened and
spread taut against the rock.

Journeys

At the end of the journey we built
another pyramid, intending
to rendezvous with the gods.
Each contributed a massive brick
and it was placed according
to his rank. At the top,
with a foot-hold in the heavens,
was our priest-king
with his mathematicians
and war-lords who planned it all.

As our energies ripened we were
driven on, remembering certain
promises that we carried in a chest.

Once, at sea, we gathered by the mast
to see an angry child, curled
head to tail, unfurl himself
as the ship rocked. Morals
spilt from his throat and sank
unfathomed, and, tongued
by faint light, he searched the sky.
It was a one-way mirror by day
he said — a gold and pink lie.

We left the chest behind — all
that we cared for was in the sky,
because of a small and swarthy
man-god we had learned to love.

We loved him for the curved
rib of his nose, and, because,
where he had walked, God sprang
from the soil like mushrooms
at a witch's heel. But now
he is staked out in the sky
with stars for nails, while we watch
stiff-necked and giddy,
and full of inarticulate belief . . .

Mushroom clouds like fairy rings
surround the earth. Forgive me —
I write hastily, in the shadow of my hand.

Nikou Church

The singers in Nikou church
shout to God, and then,
as though relenting, soothe
Him with their voices.
The church is new; the women
wear new hats — each hair
is counted on their heads,
each prayer spoken with new
love. But the singing
is old — it thrusts
forward from ancient time,
as though the world
were no more than a chain
of islands about a lagoon.
These people know that they
are good, know their God
has always served them well.
They are seldom surprised —
all the surprises are mine!
Now the women sing
spirals of high sound,
piercing as sea-birds
who discover something
strange in their midst;
the men boom like waves
meeting a reef, moving
their song towards a shore
where Te Atua awaits them.

Riemke Ensing

Chance meeting
(Hiroshima Day)

> Take the toys
> away
> from the boys

On my way to *Disorderly Conduct*
a launching of duck & worth(y) words
(a novel, otherwise) with light
refreshments
& drinks in the *Birdcage*
I encounter a young buck
springing to life
on his sky blue Suzuki
(GS450) on the corner.
I watch his legs
press & caress the wide body
and something
stirs
he smiles
under his sky blue

such "power between
his thighs"

such an ache/
a thudding ache I press
my legs

11 Novastar helmet
& I smile watching
his legs, his arms, the way
he bounces & watches
me smiling
& I think Orphée has come
riding right out of a Cocteau
movie, but the lights green
& he takes off
in another direction
entirely.

Northern Building Society Office showing Police Headquarters, Auckland

If I told you corner of Grey
and Mayoral drive just opposite
the *Carpenters Arms* and left
of Cook street where the markets are
you'd still have no idea
how this building shapes
itself squarely and not too tall
in the lee of the nineteenth century
tower telling you it's three o'clock
and the fountain tumbles over the green
copper slate brighter than summer
pollard showing off in the mirror
glass.
The only worry is the way
the sun reflects what you don't want
to see this blue day —
a concrete cloud.

Signal Yellow

The ginger in flower
is what you notice
first all yellow
the gorse up
everywhere
the yellow
brushes on the wattle
along the roadside
as you come round
the bend following
the line of water
you run across
the fog lifting the hills
in the distance almost
yellow.

From *Track with Tide Coming in*
for Suzanne & Duncan Stuart

4 Paikea Bay
How / at the just moment everything
conspires against you going
further.
Here is a cleft in the rocks.
The tide smashes, churns and runs
back again to come leaping
up / higher / spitting venom at you
clinging to the scared (scarred) rock
clawing at the flesh holding on.
A cloud bursts and you ask
who weeps for whom or why —
the sea, the sky, the rock
weeping?
and as suddenly the warmth again
on the skin as you're over
the crevice and back down
from the jagged leap
to smooth stone
beached
and summer in brittle ochre grass
danthonia & harestail and the great
bleached spiders loping along
in the bowled over wind as it stirs up
the sand skimming across the dunes
and blusters over the cliff
into the boiling frenzy
at the world's edge.
Also Pohuehue Mesembry anthenium
(so the book says) and an interesting
mix, or coastal ice
plant in sharp bright colours.

5 Home, writing
There are so many things
the poem can't do.

Where for example in this note
book scribble & drawing
these cryptic messages for later
is the smell of salt & sea
weed & the wind & the dry
grass waving from up the hills?

How now among the saturday lawn
mowers to re create the silence
of cobalt viridian green
under the breaking wave?

Fires From Chagall

for my father

shapes.   Signatures of larger worlds
somersaulting out of the window
open to trees, the plain street
outside where the rain is caught on
an open umbrella, and a fiddler
dances in a night lit up from inside
listening houses while the sky burns
and everything
is ambiguous and quite changed from the last
time you looked.

In the line you draw   such notions
grow that we hear the hiss of the sun
as he kisses the water
goodnight / and what is
might go in any direction
of loss / where legends take root
and roads become symbols
of danger.

Past is place and shape.
A house in a street with a square
of grass where you might see
the sky falling between walls

standing like trees touching
each other with darkness,
but I say nothing
of childhood when everything is
clear   and lines belong
to burnt-ochre faces in portraits
that might smile
as if the moon had passed
through a shadow
and left
night tied up
in columns of death / notices
under the arm of the evening star.

I go in to bury my father.
He is not a man
I recognize other than
images I have seen
before / his eyes are closed.

The light has gone from the lamp.
Under the tree the talking
has vanished and singing
is motionless in clouds / looking
for skies that breed on all that
detail of frown and restless waves
you fared on / at the edge of winter
when salt lines drew naked wind
straight from the sea scarring
this shore.

Autumn should have been
as simple as a Cezanne fruit
garden, but you were miles away
across oceans, migrating.
The search always for the other
side of whatever it might have been
you were looking for.

Winter falls here in summer   this year.
In your birthplace record snow

storms are broadcast, intense
cold.   Also appropriate.

Father, I should have touched you,
met whatever region of warmth was
in the colours you were before
the ice crept into the timid walls
of your room.

The picture is described.
The grey more sad than any pencil
mark can make on paper. Photographs
are left in drawers
but the image, I fear, will remain
a dream / far from
ending.   Already
I see
the beginning.

A sequence of events signalling
danger / a network to decode
and songs for a death coming
suddenly clearly among sirens
wailing in a street full
of movement and light / shades
of bizarre mimes making
pastiches for writers to make
pieces of paper with
to toss up to the sky like a flight
of so many coloured dragonflies
or the beautiful bird listening
to music starred with poems
serried as notes on a frail stave
of lines coming
together as tiny rainbows.

These pictures are the smell of a poem hung
up to dry like linen in the damp night
when sounds might break through the window
into that space where suddenly
a tear is the music stars make
in the calligraphy of trees.

The words speak for themselves
but the colour is personal / sombre
or black / depending on the gesture;
the way the earth might burn
orange or bitter as the lemon tree
very pretty and small in yellow
days when houses fall.

What matters is a sense of order;
the table under the stained window,
the rattan blind down against sun,
the mat on the floor facing
Mecca where such colours might come
from rocks and sand blowing
through bleached grass and the tree
of life / firm
and reaching to the mihrab
where the holy city
lies.

Conversations for Miro
the drawing in the poem/the poem in the drawing

1

Signs and patterns are what is common.
That line might be a flock of birds
migrating, could be the first stroke
towards saying I've changed my mind
not liking trickery, the games we play
the line we draw elaborately across
time forgetting the magic of colour and the sun
going down red over the horizon
in one fell swoop being swept off
the edge of the world and you're left
completely in the dark as to where
you are going.

A painter might draw beside you
symbols of landscape recognizably centred
as cloud in the window of the neighbour's
house   not moving though the wind blows.
A tree perhaps to shape you by   its leaves
making any one of four seasons.
These signs we decipher.   They tell
stories ripe as aubergine or persimmon
tall as any dictionary where treasure is
kept

        persimmon, n. diospyros kaki.
          American date plum
          yellow fruit becoming
          sweet when softened
          by frost / persimmon
          native of China bright
          fruits will hang on
          the tree in winter /
          persimmon deciduous
          small native to Japan
          can be in weeping
          form attractive both
          in leaf   and fruit
          after leaves have
          fallen / persimmon
          grows fifteen feet
          persimmon dios divine.

So much for words lying
their way from one book to another
way of saying here are the words, they tell
me a thing or two mostly
they are not the sound I want
to hear the wind
in branches the sun orange lush
or persimmon / dios, divine
the word has its limits
go and see the tree
put the fruit in your hand, your mouth
mix shape and form with what

you feel and see and mostly touch
and smell or taste and hear.

Let the poet draw circles
round the moon   the painter till
his garden, plant trees for us
to sit under and smile
as the wind does when it's up
to mischief and blows human flowers
into the book we could be.

2

These words are about lines scored
with burin or pen   how charcoal spirits
away the harsh imprint of winter engraved
needlesharp on the mind like poems
the lithographs of sound shaped
by a point fine as glass drawing
blood and the full crescendo of cathedral
music singing from the stained window
of the heart shaped as magic flame dressed
gayer than harlequin riding on rooster
or peacocks reaching for rainbows.

3

The poem I started is already
lost.   One day I will find it
on a sheet of paper pulled out
from a pile of books or unanswered letters.
Perhaps it will be
a bookmark showing the way
to mushroom growing or porcelain
glazes delicate as the smudge of Puzzuoli
red in a sketch where nothing is
sentimental but all lives speak
clearly as words do when they cry
from the heart without design
or drama   plainly as a flight of birds caught
in the sharp magic of black surprising
with its coat of colours.

Rachel McAlpine

Here it is

Well to get to the nitty-gritty,
here it is:
I was suddenly sick of praying
to men, for men.
That was the beginning,
the middle and the end.

Ritual: remind myself I am guilty,
wrong, and light in the head.

Orthodox theology and common sense:
yes our Father is sexless,
God is being, God is love,
yes the Holy Spirit is spirit
and Jesus being a Jew
simply had to be male
and he was kind to girls.
Yes I could alter pronouns privately,
yes I am married to God
and have no right to divorce.
Yes Man is metaphor for Woman,
yes I could work within,
yes I could wait a century
yes it is just as silly
to think of God as Woman —

yet things are right for me
when flesh and spirit agree:
I do not feel included.

One truth is that God the Father
calls mostly to men except
when he wants a cup of tea.

Te Kaha

oh well tonight or some other night
you or someone else will put
the usual proposition and I
will warm and waver and decline

there are nappies snapping
at the soggy breeze
white is the baby's
Invercargill flesh
he bites Makwini's brown breast

the conger eel has been underessed
and the shark is a white knife
wanting a woman this time

you will or will not know my want
blunt as a boulder
sleek as a butterfish

but I am a boat afloat
and I see many a fin

I could rock you in the sun
I could be babied and reborn
but I age, I rage at other men
laughing and lying at their wives
and trying the tips of their knives

offering

for months now
I have brought you nothing

but today you will see on the step
a slight grey poem
barely flecked with blood
so lightly was it caught

this purse of fur contains
bones of flute
notes of flesh
palpitation quelled

it is the only gift
for one as quick as you
despite your speed
you cannot hunt like me

still I would swallow the lot
if you rebuked my purring
if you did not stroke my neck

fancy dress

I always dressed in style
an apron, lace and
lipstick, a mortar-board and
cassock of wholesome black

but you with your small blunt words
have nibbled it all away

I crouch on the frozen clay
growing my pointed fur

I say lover, lover, lover
we both know that's a lie

you grow younger and younger
                cover me

burning the liberty bodice
OK
take off your clothes

stretch and see
how your body seems

just right
almost as if
it were made for you

your nails spring like leaves
and every goose bump sprouts
your trunk bends to the wind's
drunken massage
and your scalp goes sky high
tossing like tussock

now you notice your things
softly bumping together
and how one lip lies
delicious on the other
in a lifelong kiss

stop
this is risky
better put on your
clothes

bird-woman

this is awkward I apologise
if it hurts as I hook in

we are tail-heavy I was planned
for lighter loads

I'm taking you north Rimutakas Tararuas
it's been a hard snowy season but
you'll love it

see my cosy sticks and stones see
my clever library For Sale Rest Area
Beware of Wind

I peck off your squeal do not shake like that
you need some titbits of possum

at this level I need a superman
with your leathery head and your gristly legs
you look almost worthy

but close up you are the same
pale pulpy mixture as the rest
well you will have to do

you are cold come under my wing
I am an angel
I am a ladybird

stop whingeing please
yet I desire your voice

the snow is blind the wind bores me
and I am the only one of my kind

let me work your tongue with my claws
this is the way it is done
I need to hear my name

OK if that's your game
forget it we shall mate instead

excuse my claws it is a tricky business
must I spell this out? lie still

after all I've done I feel
wounded

my views my home my food refused
my words even my singular body

at least there are a few red
meals on your bones
you may think this is fun but for me

it's a nightmare
you've got everything
but I am lonely

first your eyes I hate
to be watched while I eat

next my beak on your tonsils
down there down there
are the words I need

how you love me or how you don't
how you miss the Olden Days
how wonderful/lousy I am as a lover

the soft bits while they are warm
and your limbs for later
safe from scavengers

you grow hard and cold
I told you you were hard and cold

now let us look at the sights
now let us fly in the sunset
light in the head
with love

From *House Poems*

xiii

the house flatters her ankles
with purple pink and green
the house prefers me to mention
spring in a soft voice often

polyanthus and peppermint
parsley and periwinkle
violet, viola, Virgina stock

rock tulip, jasmine
oreganum, angelica
forget-me-not, iris, crocus and chives

I plaited a litany of flowers
so we would have some syllables to sing
something feathery and savage
to celebrate come September

these are all the names we need
for our September song
this has always been the song
of a square yard garden in the city

x house breaking

this house has been flapping
for a nonchalant lot of years
a flag or a ponderous swan

I have a comment
of great aplomb:
I am nearly forty

but she is old beyond all shame
dancing her tango waving her apron
at every passing gale

little by little the earthquakes
loosen my nuts and bolts

ix household words

Maria, Antonia, Lisa, Mary, Kulala
it took me months to get you straight
because you change your names at will
to Adrienne, Lucia, Ana, Maria, Christine

moreover all of you
claim to be Rachel too
this I claim to believe
I too have had many names

Jigger, Robin, Fishface, Tosh and Pud
I popped them one by one
I stretch in my only name
given, earned and grown

my name divides like a bulb
and five new Rachels wait
for a playful sun

we: me and my name and address
we are not poorer for this

xii

I'm playing house
mother without father
mother without other mother
mother without children
playing playing house
with only the house to play with

I've picked my team
me and the house will win

I've Got a Poem

I've got a poem half written
like I've got a new lover
and I don't want to say who he is
yet.

Wherever it is, the poem is the centre
of the room. All the time
I am making the bed, going for a jog,

taking a shower,
the poem rings.
Can it wait? What'll I say?
A thin flame runs up my legs.

On the bus I think of other poems.
Now I have six half written.
I am a slut
with petrol in my hair.

A Good Day

Well it's been a good day for me,
a little job done, a big one started;
torso buzzing, knees vibrating
and waves of semen oozing
on their expedition south.
Is anyone a cynic on a day like this?
Shamefully old and still a child,
discovering over and over again
the cornucopic atoll
like Captain Cook on video.

Should I argue with life about that?
"No thanks, I've had one of those"?

I've got the random hots,
I like him and I've checked him out.
I try my first-class pick-up line:
"I've got a broken heart.
Would you like to autograph the plaster?"
And once again I find a skin
of polished onyx, like the surface
of my mislaid Mister Right;
his hair is red or grey or brown,
his are the shapeliest hands
I ever shook.

Look, Thoreau, we're all in time
at a certain frequency.
The iron that pleats the harbour here
is beating the icy sea
around the Falklands.
And crystals on a billion wrists
shake in time with the quartz
beneath the concrete.

I'll see him again but in between
I do my work and love it and I'd
never think of him, except
my job is poetry.
Moon spoon blue true —
never mind that. Bring me
the body of a brand new friend,
with the best cock in the world.

It's been a very good day.

Darling

A word sucks at my window,
all fluffed up with daffodils
and ducklings. "Say me! Sponsor me!
and I will wind the tight blue sky
around us in a double mummy!"

Today my heart is bloodshot,
and I feed on irony. Today Iran
expands with swords and forks,
Israel stamps its foot today,
today Muldoon is snarling in his box
and Argentina fires a load of medals.

I long to use the word I tried to swallow.
It rises in my throat
like a softened Panadol.
"Darling," I want to say, "darling."
My hand moves to the thigh

of a gentle man, and I hear
it saying "darling" —

just as the hot invisible thermal
lifting the sturdy pelican
insinuates "darling",
just as the heron's porcelain image
sits on the water's silk
with a hint of "darling".

Easily I could snuggle in
the shallow inlet of a man,
sliding on the silence wrinkled only
by the pinch of "darling, darling".

Darling is the first invasion,
darling is the word that starts a war.
I'm screeching through the heads alone,
to dumpers and rocks and wrecks and spray,
grazing the calm horizon with my work.
I plan to tackle the junta mouth to mouth.

There are so many stronger words
I want to use. Darling
will have to find another flat.

Before the Fall

After the bath with ragged towels
my Dad
would dry us very carefully:
six little wriggly girls,
each with foamy pigtails,
two rainy legs,
the invisible back we couldn't reach,
a small wet heart,
and toes, ten each.

He dried us all
the way he gave the parish
Morning Prayer:
as if it was important,
as if God was fair,
as if it was really simple
if you would just be still
and bare.

Devotions

Some are poets. Others are trumpets
with the flat eyed pizzazz of the stupid.
They humble me. I am like this, of course.

How hard it is to dance on the poplar tops
spontaneously, with fifty people looking;
to make a perfect nest, without showing off.

I have to learn how to use peacock
tails for toothpicks and vice versa,
how to be devout without losing shape,
how to read as me and not as pantomime,
crowbar, vamp, baby-doll, smart-ass or bore.

Poetry is public and costs a lot.
There is too much admiration.

Because the cheap trick works quicker,
I swear never to forget tonight's sunset
wriggling liquidly on a window, splashing
from sky to pane to retina to page
so I can hardly write for fireballs.

An eiderdown split on Greenknowe Avenue
on Friday. We were moguls for a morning,
walking ankle deep in down.
After a day, the fluff remains in only
three places: in the gutter, on a strip
of fresh tar, among the weeds at tree-base.

I don't want you to stumble tarred and feathered
from this reading. I don't want to leave you
in the gutter. Most of my words are doing
a fly-past. If some of them crash, and tangle
in your weeds, that'll do me.

As Grey as any Kitten

Never say this of me:
she was a busy man, she   ·
was an after dinner speaker.

I remember smoking my first cigarette
in a shed full of hay.
I remember a puppy I could not train
and so he had to go.
I remember instructing Prue
to fly out of a pine tree.

If you tell a girl about bleeding,
the next thing you know, she's tried it,
and prompting all her friends.
But isn't that best?
Secrets are lumpy. Try
to be silly and tasteless.

I want a hedgehog here,
but where will it go? Not with yellow
explosions in the greenery,
nor in the speckly rain.

It is the evening of influences,
very damp with rattles clapping
and hoo hoo of a truck below.
When will I forgive myself
for that man's faults?
It's killing me,
even though I constantly
declare I am alive
and as grey as any kitten.

Fiona Kidman

A Businessman's Lunch

While sitting in a restaurant, ready to close,
he told her how many books he'd written and how many
more copies than hers they'd sold,
he described with a flourish, between garlic
and dandruff, what a fabulous lay he was sure she would be,
and then recoiled —
his skin crawling like a snake through grass
like a snail retreating into its shell
or a wet sea anemone sensing danger —
when she touched his hand
(she could have sworn his penis turned inside out on the spot).

The subject of children and wives
was thoroughly aired ('I get plenty of high class sex
at home,' he murmured, 'its our minds which will enrich
this entire situation,' and then
proceeded to demolish the myth
of minds in the feminine gender.)
Children, well of course, he had four,
and that, you know, meant a lot of love,
as if twice as many children as she,
ensured twice as much love, or worse,
that possession was nine points of the law
and hers simply didn't exist at all.

They discussed the black hole
in the mattress through which they
both claimed to fall
when the nights were dark,
but when she erred, by expressing an opinion,
she suddenly saw his mattress, under a paranoiac quilt,
and knew that it would always be separate
beds for them:
she didn't need to wait for nightfall,
to know that her dark still had room
for stars, and crimson moon
rising between her knees.

Desert Fires

I.

The morning lake was ironed flat
as fresh blue linen, a heron
was wedged in a willow tree branch.
I turned away from a lover's kiss,
unwilling to plumb the heart of bliss,
for that's Pandora's box,
and I have worn memory like a shroud
too long; as with that chocolate box lake,
I cannot lift the lid,
there are evil sweetmeats
in its depths.

II.

I did not know that the road south
would be so unsafe. Still
both victim and plunderer, seduction
was imminent. The hills lay like breasts,
the valleys opened like thighs, sister Sappho
joined me as I plucked each bush,
wild purple heather, downy toi-toi hair,
my hands bled from the rose bush thorns
yet still I gathered their scarlet hips,
I could feel their shape against my mouth:

III.

I travelled on, the desert grew dark,
a strange cloud blotted out the world,
approaching cars warned me of the peril beyond,
with full-blown headlights at height of day:
then I saw the tongues of fire licking the plain.
Sisters, we consume and are consumed,
every country has its heart of darkness
and every heart its core of fear.
So I passed beyond the fires
and on the home strait run,
I told myself,
it all seems safe enough again.

Pact for Mother and Teen-ager

Girl, we've quarrelled
in a motel in a strange town.
It's 2 a.m. and tomorrow
I'm due to drive north all day
on the holiday we've planned
this six months past.
If you were a lover,
I'd have thrown you out;
if you were your father,
I might have had a bitter-sweet
reconciliation. But as you are
my child, I watch you sleep
tangled in bedsheets and tearstains,
and try to plan the shortest way
out of town.

Earthquake Weather

For three days now, the air
has been quiet and still.
Yesterday, a vase walked across
the mantelpiece. A friend and I
have traced the fault line
along a map. It is very close.
There is neither sun, nor yet rain,
and the wind has departed too.
The crickets have stopped singing
and the childrens' quarrels grown bitter.
We wait sealed in this
grey vacuum.

And when we went to bed
last night, the moon slanted
between the curtains (yes,
we still have a moon),
catching your white smile
in a dazzling glitter. We
who have known rage and lust,
regrets and promises, have come

to understand love. I was afraid
that you were about to devour me.
I wish this weather
would break soon.

Taupo writers' school
for my father

At mother's house your pictures
of this place hang on the walls colours
soft as tissue the wash of the water
in the paint reflecting these

mists and oh the sky over the water
is darkening the waves on the lake
sharpen like tousled lace the hem
of my shift   the spiked

cabbage tree rears its head
above
   the edge of the windowsill level with the heads
of my quiet students scratching

their verse it always seemed to me
that you shouldn't have put that bird
right at the forefront the rocks
are better and more difficult

to climb at evening well it's
impossible not to think of you (here) old
man now that you're dead and your
late drawings oh yes the light

on the lake the wind shifting
the tops of the waves and the night
leaning in on me   it's been
a bright day beneath the mountains

Made Over

My seams are fragile
tear easily in the bedclothes.
Breasts snag like broken toenails
on loose threads: head blanketed
against you

I dream   clear air
curled fingers unprising you:
find empty space
break patterns.   Patches
and mends: holding fast.

Makara Beach, Spring

It's this skin of happiness that holds
me together. Like an olive round an anchovy's
body. More loosely, like Maggie's neck
collected in folds over her collar bone
sliding about, no special grip on the world.
A dog's life all right. But god, it's good, beside
the sea collecting wild flowers and weeds
of new zealand. Blue eyed daisies, white as foam
and dark as the sea's centre, the middle's
what counts, and yellow, there's yellow
flora all over the place. I've even got you
collecting the encroaching cream off
the land, and a smudge of silver edged
leaf. A heron
bows, arches, stalks across
stones. A bunch of overland cyclists stand
aside, smile. Indians picnic in the shade
of a cliff. A Vietnamese child lies down
waiting to be rescued on the round
rocks. A tide of gorse
flows over the hills flushed at the seams
with orange broom. We agree to share botulism
if the crayfish roll at the tearooms
should fail us. Well yes. This is certainly

short enough to be happiness.
The morning's a ball
of silk unwound about us. You gather
it back with me at its centre.

From *Going to the Chathams*

On Te Whaanga lagoon's flatbed
the teeth of shark 55 million
years old wash towards my gum-
booted feet long pale blues

excellent specimens or dark & sharp
like fragments of fired bone snagging
against the fluted shore wind
whipping over this long drawn-out

extraction from the shallow surge
beyond the swans with white
underwings raised over the banks
of flounder here on the beach

they call Blind Jim it's easy
to believe no people exist
the ancient porcelain of the sky
envelops the wasteland a chance

the Bristol will not retrieve me
but cold bites hard at the ankle
& these harsh these beautiful islands
are for leaving I pack the old fangs

in the pocket of my jeans   listen
already for the morning plane await
lift-off   newspapers   time
mattering   & believable acts again

At Owenga

the schoolmistress
in the woollen cardigan
sits on the beach
with her eyes riveted
to the horizon
waiting for the barge
of sheep to come
from Pitt

'sometimes they come and sometimes
they don't,' she says.
it's saturday. she can wait
all day, or all weekend
if she wants
till the children
come again.

The Newsmakers

for Fay Weldon

On the blue screen
the woman from overseas
looks round and warm and earthy.
Her looks are deceptive. I think
she is saying one thing and meaning
another.
So do I, but then I
am tense and frail and sleepless
from a night of too many words.
Let us talk of husbands, says the interviewer,
in our small chat beforehand. The woman
laughs. Mine is twelve thousand miles away,
she says. I can say anything
I like. Can't I?

I say nothing. There is nothing
to say. I know
I will smile
and get it right.

My father taught me
to collect birds' eggs and blow
their yolks into a bowl,
to cradle the outer shells
on cottonwool, so that we could view
the colours
through glass. I place myself
in the chair, drain the centre,
expose the shell. The cameras
roll. See
how hard
I am.

Elizabeth Smither

Here come the clouds

Here come the clouds the same as last June
Puffy like the breasts of birds, one . . . two . . . three . . .
They have circumnavigated the world
Birds heavy from flight, home again

A year has passed. Now they fill the sky
Thicker and thicker having no other place to go
What is the end of navigation then? They seem
Swollen as though their arteries of air

Ached from memory as well and
Dilated their hearts so they come
Weighed with longing for their homeland
And here they are. Is this it then?
This empty sky, waiting.

First holiday under canvas

Gulls come under the canvas and herrings
Lie between the sheets. We stand on our heads
Caught in a white horizon flapping to the beat
Of waves and wind. We are brown with anger
From the sun. A great weariness that afflicts
Soldiers before battle (the tents are up, ditches
Dug to please the general, a mimosa spray
Hangs from the roof but we are not at home)
A fear greater than death is life, the passing
Of it, how it goes. Our gestures are the size
Of insects. Today, I, a young subaltern
Bathing in a stream (the cannons are far
Off yet, you hear them rumbling) lifted a fly
Drowning on its back and hurled it into air. It flew
Away without faltering. I envied it.

Great grandmother

Great grandmother was set on fire
By a birthday cake. Grandfather waved
The frieze and the candles caught it
Great grandmother fell in a pile of bones.
They poured coffee over, then brandy down.
Great grandma revived to waves of adoration.

But the panthers were around her slippers
The cubs of all the cats on invisible leashes.
They damaged her pompoms because you were jealous
(She was taking grandfather away from you.)

The Frog Prince

(after reading the analysis by Bruno Bettelheim)
That night when he lay on my pillow
The engorged face of my father
Shone from the mirror.

The second night I was meek at table
They noticed the change in my behaviour.
I hurled the frog at the wall.

I will not serve, I decided. I never cared
For the ball at the bottom of the well.
I will leave if necessary.

Today a prince with a migraine
Wakes beside me.
His other arm encircles.

City girl in the country

The rooster crows like someone being sick.
How Nature stinks! The fecund pots
Of time-embalming herbs visibly
Eat what sun there is embalming us.

The proper oils, the proper bread
Seem offerings to a beetling god
Whose hair sprouts under the flagstones
Whose orisons arise in fleas.
The busy ant, pernicious wasp
Devour their mutual hemispheres.
The girl in the garden calls out 'Shit!'
Aimlessly pulling out the weeds.

At the Tuki Tuk motel

Towards morning a motorbike wakes me like a bird.
The grey is being dragged from the room. Twice
In the night I went to the drapes and looked out:
Gravel and night lights, a soundless frost.
Hard to imagine you're a traveller, hard to make
A home of it, away from home, left with
The bare pins, the sound of a bike, not even a bird.

Orangeade with an American at Brighton

The pavilion is a seraglio
A distinct slap
In the eye of a wife.

In the kitchens
You may have noticed
A fat plaster rat.

We pause here
To stir the sugar in
Orangeade leaves a scum.

The cost of all
Those chandeliers
The refusals of ladies in drawing rooms.

What was the point of
Thirty-six entrees
Sauces for old venison?

Even the bamboo
Did you observe
Was made of wood?

To compete with lacquer
Bland wickedness
Must have pained the ladies.

While the men could drown
Debts of corpulence
In the dining-room.

And now the photos
Of my wife
Left behind in Boston.

The legend of Marcello Mastroianni's wife

All summer in the shallow sea
She lay on a lilo waiting
Dangling a hand, primed to embrace
And bless the demi-god.
She would cook from the freezer
Breasts of pasta, sauces like milk
Spoon-feed him, flirt
Mountainously and save herself.
In bed while she ministered
Territories of herself she spoke
Into the darkness the litany she'd learnt:
Whales, dolphins, the dove-like sea.

Temptations of St Antony by his housekeeper

Once or twice he eyed me oddly. Once
He said Thank God you're a normal woman
As though he meant a wardrobe and went off
Humming to tell his beads. He keeps
A notebook, full of squiggles I thought, some
Symbolism for something, I think I've seen
It on lavatory walls, objects like chickens' necks
Wrung but not dead, the squawking
Still in the design, the murderer running.
He's harmless, God knows. I could tell him
If he asked, he terrifies himself.
I think it makes him pray better, or at least
He spends longer and longer on his knees.

Casanova in midwinter

Along the empty promenade
The spa-like waters of the sea
Pour themselves like a glass
Flung down by a slattern.
Asked to undress the chambermaid
Removed only the essentials
The embrace was hindered by
A body steamed by prohibition.
Furtiveness even when it accommodates
Cannot oblige in the end
Better a crossing in the troughs
Than staterooms with peeling paint.
The sun can be bought. It is a matter
Of a game of belote with a stranger
Or the chambermaid's life savings
In exchange for certain renovations.

Casanova and the residues of indifference

At the amusement parlour
The fellatio clowns
Taking balls into their mouths
With the o of choirboys
Singing Palestrina

Remind me of calendars
Circled around and dropped clothes
Satin lamps, the latest books
And the night turned back
Like a quilt.

Filing catalogue cards

"When pregnancy fails"
"When the winds blow"
"When tigers fight"
"When trees were green"

Between the cards slip tigers trees
The child blown away by wind
Each desire on the white card
Is a perfect picket fence

While through the cards the rod
Holds the world together
Keeping apart the green child
From the windblown tiger.

A skyful of stars

Look up and they're word perfect
As you always knew: equations, theorems
The molecular structures like winding stairs
And the explanation of plants, their roots
That may be of air or earth, wherever
The desirable water is, a loving gaze.

First speech lesson

Sister Teresa bends over me
As I lie with my head on a book
After we've danced to music
Articulate gestures, opening the throat.
Poets are sensitive, she says
I've come so I can read better
The upward and downward glide of the voice
The force of the excitor.
At the bottom of my feet the garden
Receives the palatals of the rain
And the mute statue of Christ
Points to his rib reserve heart.

Shakespeare virgins

for Fiona

The English examiner of speech
Forgave our accents but not
Our Shakespearian virginity.
Could we admit it
Some towns had no cathedral
No roistering market place?
We had never plunged into
Emotion larger than words
The words running with it
Never taken part in or witnessed
A footfight: word against meaning
Each with flashing daggers.
Somehow he made it sound
Sadder than the old virginity
Discarded near the almshouse
That Shakespeare might have noticed
Only *en passant*.

Male poets with small handwriting

Why do none of the male poets I know
Write anything but small and straight
Cagey I'm inclined to call it.

None of them flows all over the place
With swoops up and down and fat lettering
If they cross out it's always neat.

Is it their awareness of words is so great
Like handling hot rocks from a thousand feet
This is the reason they write in white coats?

Certainly mine runs away like a goat
And the poem is held at the end of a chain
Lest the goat gets into the vegetable patch.

Each word as they pluck it feels chosen and right
In their spidery writing close to its fellows
For it's soon joined by some other stripling.

It's like a camp call-up.   Stick close and tonight
There'll be a singsong and bonfire
And all of these words will sizzle together.

Whereas I'm reining in a most fearful scribble
In which at the heart
Words lie under the trampled grass.

La ligne donnée

The exercise in observation where
Several people decide
In their own detail how
A girl going through a door
Catches the corner of her dress in it:
La ligne donnée
And what follows
In the altercation that breaks out

Didn't you see how
The skirt swirled, the material being full
How her hand brushed and caused it
One fold shot forward, it was her gait
At once jerky and feminine . . .

Leave the room at this juncture
The poem will follow.

A question of gravity

All day we fought against the sky
And in theatres aimed towards the gods
Spun on our toes our eyes high on a wall
Above gravity addressed our purest thoughts.

All night we lay weakly giving in
Held someone close if someone was around
Murmured a prayer and looked towards the roof
Dreamed and straightened out our backs.

The O in Shakespeare explained

Sometimes a writer turns
His eye to the whole of his subject
Or a whole subject apart from it
O is the word for it.

This book against a stream, a flood
A sky of stars that process
Any digression as long as it is large
O is the word for it.

A hundred thousand blades of field
And it held while in all detail
A wheel of birds that sagas make
O is the word for it.

And Shakespeare's head beginning to ache
For sure the play is a sandwich
And slippery as eel or heart
O is the word for it.

The tiny weight of the soul

At death the body diets by an ounce or less
Some energy kept its heaviness afloat
And weighed with it, like a hat.

Now for scales of doubt, being the best
A measurable difference but not an excess
Like humouring a Thomist with an interest rate

Is enough to pierce the ratio as though
Some last postscript of a proof was left
As lightly as the dropping of a glove.

The Creative Writing Course Faces the Sonnet

Something formal, say a silver jug
By Cellini or espaliering apples
Can be approached by two methods:

Usefulness: Cellini was known for spouts
And espaliering apples is practical
In a narrow garden with one wall

Or envy: Who gave the popes these millions
Who left these fossils of great beauty
Which still fruit in irony?

Sue Harlen

Pelorus

The entrance is deceptive
marked by rough water
and wind funnelling
from the Tasman through
the North-East channel
where mountain chains
break like memory
into deep time.

A slow journey
among the drowned ranges:
inlets branching to
unseen bays. We
steer as if secure,
yet in the mist
outlines of ridge
and summit blur.

The solution is here
in the blueprint
of foam, the script
of light on water,
obscure skylines
stark and cryptic
as the landmarks
of a dream.

Bait

I dreamed that
you stabbed me
with the long knife
you use for fish.
There was no pain;
we fish feel nothing.
A clear liquid
flowed from the wound.

The dream said
it was a way
of being bled.
A fish screams
with no sound,
twitches, gapes
in frantic, cold-eyed
fear of dying.

You dangled love
like squid
on a steel hook,
the oldest rod
and line in town,
breaking-strain unknown;
gear guaranteed
for big game.

Now who is bait?
Who reels
the spangled night?
I set out late,
watch the boat write
luminous trails
and let black skylines
steer me home.

Killing Time

remember how
there used to be
a time lag
13 minutes and
9 point 4 seconds
to decide this
is it sweetheart
or maybe its only
egg on the screen
well its wonderful
what they can do

with chips these
days that computer
can suss it now
in 4 minutes point
2 seconds you may
not even have time
to read thi

Hook Hours
For my father

I
— Fishing is
a matter
of hook hours —
you said and
cast your line
out to the
horizon.
We never
missed a break,
even trolled
the long wake
for Kahawai
as we ran
the channel.

I learned to
read the lines,
to wait in
a half-dream
on the slack
tide for signs
of Groper
mouthing the
bait to bite;
played line to
the big one
when it ran

deep to shake
the hook's grip.

Between us
we pulled in
more than our
share over
all the bright
lost seasons.
This summer
the Tuna
are running
early, but
I have spent
my hook hours
casting the
past for you.

II
You never heard;
thought it was
just a sea-bird
calling as the hook
sank. You pulled
me in again
bleeding silver
on the end of
your green line.

My mouth is torn;
I'm the one
that got away.
I'm the one
that bit back —
remember that.
Pack up your
gear, old man,
the tide has turned.

You won't know me;
I have sung you
onto the rocks,
sung you
a slow drowning;
strapped to the mast
you won't get past,
I haven't finished
with you yet.

III
I knew it
was not true
when they said
how you died,
for I saw
you fight in
a black sea
and sink, full
fathom five,
anchored to
an ebb tide.

I have fished
at the head
of Pelorus;
my line dragging
too heavy
for the lead,
snagged in your

jawbone or
your cold, red
eye. Holding
onto you
my hands bled.

I do not
want to bait
the dead where
they wait far
back in the wake,
or turn in
their deep bed.

I have let
go of you
to the soft
swell. When you
dream a world
dream me well.

Heather McPherson

To the Poet who Called Himself a Fox among the Hens

Remember Maui.   He thought
to snatch immortality
till a fantail laughed
and Hine closed her thighs.

Remember Gwion.   He changed
to hare, fish, bird and grain —
and Cerridwen became bitch,
otter, falcon — and black hen.

Chant from the Goddess stand

I have been humankind
have seen more years
than I care to count
in the handled showcase stand
the shadow behind the man

ignored or ridden or raised
a hen in a wire coop
what I have been defaced
what I shall be
is at stake

who can be your own

She who has hatched the future and reflects it
   she who has clung to her vestment, never coerced
      she who has been reborn and discards old skins

She of the beak sharp mind and lidded sight
   she of the porcelain smile, propped in family plate
      she of the stringy arms and unlaced laugh
         she in the dark

She in a flowery dress and she in worker's gear
  she in a bride mask, smiling
    she in a scar frieze, staring
      she in a gorgon's glare and elaborate sleeves
        she on the roadside
          she in the refuge
            she in the window waving a white-gloved hand

She who was laid bleeding on white sheets
  she who thrusts a wet head into the world
    she who has sung a step ahead of climbers
      she who moves silently, silently, barely seen

She who is Nine white seasons, she who is Three
who is Rake and Rage and Tender, Holder of feeling
Keeper of the first found Key, who is abundantly
the Lovers, and the Separation Mountains, Midwife
of the dying and the Dead, who spreads the Glad
Watch open, for living Breath . . .

  This is her journey, this is her journey
  this is the journey of the woman with the bound head freed
  this is the journey of the seabird landbird daughter sage
      explorer inheritor creatrix
  this is her long trek, this is her saga
  this is her dream and her assumption
      and her apotheosis
    since she reclaimed her self
      I am She is I am

    who was adjunct and opponent
    who was possession and white jug
    who was vessel mould made soulless
    now I have crossed the shallows
      now I have come back
      I Am I Am I Am

Close-up

A woman inside an enormous sunhat
scrapes at a hillside. Below her a string road
winds round the corner and out of sight. Above
her, a storm mass creeps across the sky.
    She tussles, she tugs at the earth.
White hairy roots lie crumpled at her feet.
Overhanging tussock cuts her hands.
    She is clearing a space to paint on.

A New Year Terminal

A caller thumps at the door . . . her workshirt
hangs sweat-darkened, she blots the unfilled sun
above the hills . . . her haversack holds causes, her
aura joins old aches and refugees . . . sisters, and
this parliament . . . a chopper shakes the greenery,
a pale horse flees behind the sun-dazed walls . . .
            and the Sugarloaf mast sharpens,
                a glitter outline
        and bees fly, furry-bagged, above the roof,
and clamber up jostling grass . . . all is moving,
and carries back, the myths of past and future . . .
the next great heave bares stalks and branches
                for revolt

Crossing Sydenham Park

Crossing Sydenham Park to meet the trees
I caught their current . . .
        shore shore   shore shore
Wind lights a cyclone in the foliage, young
oaks fling their leaves . . . Under a rag washed sky
trunks wrench themselves, stump-legged, into March,
this hot wet month blows bees awry, and sense . . .
Small black bodies crawl in grass, in dirtworks,
my feet squelch on the cricket pitch, the grounds

stretch, sheetlike . . .
    shore shore   shore shore
  The pale woman, she with the shut jaw and white
gown, would have relished trees, the walk . . . her talk
was hearty, her loving hard . . . A branch like a breaker
sweeps its leaf crowd sideways . . . Down by the pensioner
flats, pigeons peck small heaps of crusts . . .
    shore shore   shore shore
  A coffin always small, the last sight long.
Under a tall tree cloister the body walks . . . perception
shifts, Cybele's million bee tracks swing, the brain
tips from infinity to a daisy stalk . . . white petals,
the pink vertices emerge, quick jars of love and
pain . . . Magpies yodel, a sweet curdle, in the wind . . .
    shore shore   shore shore
  A seagull fleet moors, halfmoons, in the grass,
the rearguard cock their wings and paddle forward . . .
a school bell rings. Somewhere over the skyline and
Nazareth House high fences, a flat collects lost
bearings . . . paintings, breast bowl, photographs . . .
crossed hands that hated bedrest . . . They circuit
the white cauldron where healing stirs, and
changes . . .
    shore shore   shore shore
  Birds break flight, the sky droops, spits.
Thin arms, the powerlines, string empty staves across
it . . . the park's a tilting barge while trucks crank
whooping past . . . Crosscurrents over death, as love . . .
the living city rocks its elements, a woman, her
living absence . . .
    shore shore   shore shore
                           for Perl 1979

Theology and a Patchwork Absolute

                      Time and again,
time and again I tried to write a goddess song.
Now that I have fleshed the lyric tongue a poem
stirs. It breaks from its inhabitants. Red shapes

blaze in the patchwork quilt. Here are two women
naked on a bed.
　　　Such proximity is heretical and a sin
to theologians and borough councillors. Their voices
shake the boardrooms. Bearded ones look stonily
from blazoned coats of arms. Thick carpet corridors
choke between the walls.
　　　And we strip absolution. We have become
our own theologians and counsellors. Our skins are
moon washed. Our laughter escalates. If sometimes
we hear Unclean Unclean we ascribe it to the
mythical leper, mournful behind his bell. From
driftwood fire to loft we heal the biblical
landscape.
　　　We have unpicked the spiral staircase.
We have pieced out a goddess ancestry from digs
and neglected pottery to risk her gifts.
　　　One is the faculty of clearing a Selective
Hard of Hearing. Libraries and presses yield
their fast. Shelves inch out to accommodate new
limbs. A poem holds the shell of an inner
chamber.
　　　Voices between the breasts. Satin
and seersucker edged with feather stitch. Arms
that slide down forearms. Yellow plums.
Serenities.
　　　Proximity of old lyric tongues and this.

(Having seen past the gods,
their power, we make a goddess,
ours . . .)

　　　　　It comes in a flat box
　　with instructions and an illustrated front.
　　　　Tapemeasure snaking greenly
　　round her, the cover model, immaculately
　　　　　　toothed and coiffed
　　　　　points at the product
　　　　　　triumphantly —
　　　　　　a substitute body
　　　　　　　for home sewers.

It resembles a museum case escapee —
 "the armoured torso"
  to protect —
or a scold's — bridle
  mortify —
   the flesh . . .
 Such anonymity
  is scope.

The goddess unapproachable . . .
 a shape in the maker's hands
  before clothes
  make the class, or fantasy —
  before a woman
  sews herself in place.

Christina Conrad

                    i have plaited my horns
                       i am lying here
                        will you come
                    will you ever come to me
          have you caught any fishes in your net
                 once on the way to your place
             i seed a big fish with a shining eye
      i was walking to your place over stony road
        i was walking in painted skirt decorated
                     with savage stitches
              my breasts little and tentative
                yet full of milk for my child
                      i was walking to you
              i seed a fish with a shining eye

                          i am dark
                          dark dark
                    a dark wolf strolling
              a dark wolf stroking the grass
                          i am dark
                            dark
             a dark wolf wearing a rainbow

remember when we made a fire at half moon bay
we taked bread and walnuts
and banana passion fruit
you and robin got pippies
we made a fire
you sat next to me
i could not feel you
i went and sat near the women chewing nuts
their breasts hidden
i could not feel the fire
i could not feel the fire
i could not feel myself
you held out a walnut to me
i bit it out of your hand savage
i feeled you
you seed me
a slow flame ran over me

i cannot paint this woman
with your penis rising out of her head
her finger nails are white
mine are black
this fig tree has thorns
there is none light
there is none light
this fig tree has thorns
her clitoris is dark red
the hill is burnt
i cannot paint this woman with your penis
rising out of her head

i had a dream
of a chair i had made
its back was like moving water
it had two knobs like acorns
they opened
inside was a scratched drawing of a little christ his
penis lying long
i feeled this dream over me
i did not know what it meant
i wanted to paint a little religious man with a basket
of bread
walking by a river with big stones and fish shewing
i wanted to paint women with vaginas and bosoms
our landlady told us to go
we could not find a place
i went with my child on a big boat
a storm came
we stayed with a man
i did not like him
the next day the storm went
we found a house
lying below the road
it was here my second child was born

i am thinking of the ram on my mothers vegetable dish
the ram was glued to the side
a single fanatics eye looking out
the dish loomed white and terrible
i always watched the ram
i seed past the ram
all the while the dish stayed white and unchanging
my mother rising above it
a caged bird

i loved my mother
i thinked all the world was in her face
i used to go into her wardrobe
and swing on her dresses in the dark
i would feel her face on mine

i have made in clay and painted
a woman
and two men
the woman in the centre
small
her face dark and fierce
her vagina in full flower
yet gasping
her hand huge
clenched
her foot
her eyes shut
darkness beside her
the man
his face falling
his mouth full
his chin resting on his arm
a cross
his palm a red cave
its you on each side of me
in darkness
me turning away from you
sparks around our heads
in a pattern of tears

your mother gave me flowers with red stamens
and spotted stems
six brown eggs

i have made you twice
with me in the middle
to be baked in the little brick kiln
you made your mother
by the mandarin tree

Dinah Hawken

A solution

From either stand point
personal/political
it is
actually
all that's needed
— the right
tilt
of the head
on the shoulders.

If you
slowly
very slowly
lift your head
from this page

do you feel it?

It's the pivot
of possibilities
the affluent
plane
finely angled
between
arrogance and shame.

Choosing Horses

Wellington is windless and wildly
blue. The house has newly painted red
doors that match the shoes I bought last night.
All night I've been swimming a huge
deeply flowing river, watching a swirl
of teeming insects or filling in
statistics on recreation.
The kids are inking Pac-man over

everything. He's munching food, faces,
words and other Pac-men. Two friends
are coming this weekend: one serene
as Krishnamurti has a new man
who wears just one earring, the other
is unrelentingly herself. I know
women too frightened to leave their own
houses, sleeping beauties. Don't for Christ's
sake wait for any prince to show up.
Fashion one from a rib or sling up
onto the wild horse rearing in your
mind. These words won't be slapped down to size
they're putting on their blue shoes, mounting
their red horses and swirling out unrelentingly over everything.

Balance

1.

I had just chosen this theme
when the global situation
suddenly deteriorated. The whole gang
started moving in — the Cubans,
the Syrians, the terrorists,
the big boys, of course, toying
with their accumulated ammunition.
I backed down into a thin,
very beautiful woman, willing
to offer anything they wanted
— a miniature daffodil, some sort
of love, to accommodate the blunt end
of their strategies, plans, a glove —

when a quiet and terrifying poet,
Adrienne Rich, stepped in.
She stood there with an M16
at her back. I lay
dreadfully apart on the carpet.
Then her voice began unfolding

like layered rock in the afternoon sun,
precision glancing off, in striking bands,
and it was clear
that she offered me a future
— a precarious one, with a constantly
human body and two huge wings.
And I remembered
what they planned to hack from our dark
gently breathing lands.

2.

So I take hold of this poem
which has come from the front.
From the newspaper. From a narrow crack
in a stack of exploded concrete.
From the hand of a paratrooper, reaching out
through the crack to a friend, in Lebanon.
From the voice of a marine, pleading
under collapsed stories of man-made rock,
'Don't leave me here.' And what I ask
from far below my own life,
as the rescue work goes on, and what
we must know in this time of crisis, yes,
and grief, hunching towards the best,
most ambitious dead end of all, is where
are the women, where exactly are we?

3.

We have been watching here
for years, and we know, that power
split from the source of its own
body and breath is of a mind
to divide everything else on earth, even
the simplest thing, for a brief
desperate show of brilliance; and that we,
crouched, still, in the hills
of our bodies, are most needed
when we are most
revolted. And we don't know,

living as we do in the decadence
of division, whether we can stand
binding love into this accuracy, and
if we do, whether we can hold it there.

Testing the East River

He said it wasn't a real river and ever since
I've been suspicious and insecure. Bet you've noticed
how everyone is using 'paranoia', even
Harry who's so damned straightforward, so familiar
with his own banks. Before we landed in this country
I dreamt about the river — one live green strip and then
a grey slaggy one, in diagonal striations,
reflecting the city, a dead heat. Explaining too
its fascination. We slung our ice-skates up over
our shoulders and went down to have fun. That's the telling
thing. And when we did arrive the sun sprinkled surprise
on the water which surged like earth's other true fluids
carrying yachts, handling tankers, smoothly, usefully.
Then to be told out of the blue that it wasn't a real
river. He's too precise that kid with his love of maps.
No, it doesn't bubble clean out of the ground, or growl
down out of the mountains as rivers should, but it flows
from Harbour to Sound and back which is O.K. with me.
But you see, they could sneak out while I'm dreaming of home
and install a clear blue version, with electronic
acceleration, and they could show the complete scheme
live on T.V. where it'd win a national award,
and we, Harry the kids and I, we'd just pack up and
come home, hoping like hell they wouldn't follow.

Walking Together, Fifth Avenue

Strolling from the best neighbourhood come
two women whose middle-aged faces
have been infallibly fashioned
grandmother by grandmother. One wears

a mauve coat, a gay red hat, and holds
a walking stick loosely in her hand.
She might in other circumstances
have carried a small white dog. What is
striking is her red smiling mouth set
on a secret angle, delighted.

What you notice about the other
is not the dark colour of her shoes,
her skin or her thin uniform, what
is striking is how her eyes level
cold along this road, and the hard fact
of her mouth. What you must discover,
stopping suddenly, looking back, what
you must fall for, is the formula,
the knack, of carrying your own head
like that — resolute, accurate, still.

Writing Home

2.

It's October and the deciduous trees
and the homeless people I know are wrenching

me into their exposed tenacious lives.
Across the river, which still endlessly

saves my soul by running off with it
towards the harbour, a crane is dangling its steel claw.

Winter swings down so fast on Martha, Steve and George.
Already they're in their thick coats. Already

they need to dream of spring while I'm dreaming of them
trying to bring them directly and deeply inside.

The trees though go on as usual accepting everything
like the holy creatures we'd love but fear to be.

Let's excel ourselves, they say, let's set the world alight
before the long clenched collective withdrawal.

7.

Even though we are here together in the same room
my words to you are framed

the way the volcano Taranaki is framed
in the print beside the window, the way

Taranaki was tamed — to near extinction — in the arms
around my childhood and hastily re-named

in this tactful second language. Egmont. Taranaki.

looming over us

the way the stark
delicate city
is looming over us

beginning to steam

the way
Fujiyama is beginning to steam

about to break

the way my sheer ancient restraint must break
if I rise

if here   waist deep   in mid-life
when I see that I can't survive, I rise

if I refuse this time to dive
and I rise

the way a tidal wave itself must accumulate and rise

massively, weightlessly   refined and ablaze

before it folds
thunders in
and eventually, subsides.

14.
You have to enter an empty room to find
what you want is not there.

                        Mother has gone upstairs
to quieten the youngest child and when she returns
she must sleep because she is ill and may be dying.

                     Somewhere, far off,

shafting from round an old cellar door, is a deep,
almost tangible blue light, but when by chance

you discover it, journeys and years later, and see that even
a glimpse is more fulfilling than you ever imagined,

you don't open the door, not because you can't, but because
you don't want to, because what you have longed for

is too extraordinary, it would be too absorbing, and you're not
yet ready for it, and you may never be.

16.
Bev, at last the park is a high green room.
All weekend I have been with friends who see,

and show that they know, how bleak things are.
It is a huge relief. This morning, the sun over Queens

has turned the river into a field of undeniably
light diamonds and the bright oaks,

which seem to have risen out of it,
look calm enough to waste the whole day

handling their excitable new leaves.
I wish you could have seen the speed

with which Martha, a mass of silver bangles
shining on her wrists, sneaked the last

chunk of chocolate ice cream out of the trash,
off the stick, and into her old mouth.

Traces of Hope

1. After browsing in a large bookshop

If we could all get together — just once — like a sea
of winter trees flicking into leaf, then choosing
the right swami, the right economic theory, the right diet

wouldn't matter, since any particular one
would be wedged against the nature of things
and it's the nature of things I'm opting for,

even if her bed is so dishevelled,
so thrashed about on, it's not clear
whether she is dreaming here or not.

2. After the usual night's sleep

So here we are in our cars in the hospital parking lot
waiting for our life-long companions to emerge
when the wave we have hoped for begins

to gather in the Pacific, in a strange
evolutionary way, and we don't notice it. Or
like the characters in a political cartoon

we are totally preoccupied baring
and clenching our teeth. Either way
the traffic drones on, with us in it

and it's only in dreams that we are swinging
from place to place on a rope through the sky
we love because it has no sound and is blue.

3. After T'ai-Chi Chuan in the park
When you come down to it we have nothing much.
Just our bodies. And while they continue to rust
and shudder living in them all of a piece

is the sought-for arrangement, one
that every so often we become — with unearthly
perceptions — with hair's breadth composure.

4. At the Kandinsky exhibition
If drifting along this unusually empty
layer I begin to become unbound, I can arrange a tryst
in a calmer compartment. A triangle appears. How whole it is, lit

by mercurial red light. And the cones! So reasonable and peaked.
Shelves are built instinctively, but adhere to certain rules.
Round, tuneful, wistful things are filling them, landlocked.

I'm off the rails and need to rise. A classically sad
tone is where I'll have to fall to: then I will depart
in reams and reams of arrows, swerving out and suddenly up.

Both

1.
On the verge of another global
breach and in
an essential way
optimistic since eggs

have been laid like tiny light bulbs
on the upwardly
curving fibre of a frayed
palm leaf in the Colorado desert

2.
On the verge of another
global breach and in an essential
way inconsolable
since eggs have been laid
like tiny light bulbs
on the upwardly curving fibre
of a frayed palm leaf
in the Colorado desert

3.
Both optimistic
and inconsolable, inconsolable and
optimistic

Winter. New York.

Four stories high with the scent
of the Christmas tree, and with sunlight

slanting through ferns, and with the river
outside like a mass of silver flags

waving to say we *are* the sea, not just
a tired limb of it, I can ignore

the hoot and roar of everyone getting there
first, and fast, which hasn't stopped

once in a year, and the hard,
intractable facades that take up so many

windows: I can be at home for a while,
high over the harbour, working a small

object from native wood, or bone,
flaking it slowly, and intently, into shape.

The Facts,

they refuse, point blank, to take responsibility
for themselves, for us, or for any other damned thing.
But they come, all the same, and screw their ugly knuckles
into our arms, and threaten to hover if they don't
get our attention. This last bunch rode in like Big Red
and his boys from Albuquerque. Remember? Here was
the quietest State Park in New Mexico, by far. Then,
black sleeveless leather and chicks in the side-cars. Truly,
I'd give anything for peace. I would. Except perhaps,
my life. Or my kids. Or the flicker of life itself.
'Stanford researchers have made an artificial womb,'
blurts the first one. 'You are too blatant, and too tactless
to come here' I snap back, longing for the primitive
art in leaves, for spring, and the lift of seeds. 'It is now
possible,' remarks another, 'to inseminate
either a woman, or an egg, with pre-selected
male-determining sperm. And,' it goes on, 'in India
amniocentesis followed by the abortion
of female foetuses is rapidly increasing.'
'That's enough,' I scream. 'You're ganging up and I'm losing
my spirit, my sense of humour.' 'Do you know,' they ask
unmoved, 'that a woman in North America has
a fifty-fifty chance of keeping her uterus?'
'Stop,' I gasp, 'for God's sake stop,' which is just what they won't
do. The researchers, I mean, and the surgeons, coasting
on and on up the main line, brilliant, sleek, impressive,
carving through the soft hills, breaking the silence, on and
on, towards the place where life begins, needing to be
the first there, to take charge from the start, believing it
possible, refusing to stop, refusing to doubt

Living With, and Without, Expectation

The instant that I wait
for the words
in your next letter

with the exact flair
that the tree
below my window

standing suddenly
in snow
awaits the first

precise impressions
of spring,
then,

I'm leaning against
a state
which all the ancient

texts and eager western
gurus are handling
with varying amounts of care,

enlightenment,
and imperceptibly
I'm slipping into it

Joanna Paul

Four Poems From Imogen

probe prove probing probable probity
                                        proboscis
I probe
she you Imogen probe probes probe
        the forefinger
        the extended forefinger
                            touching

each   each thing
I at the nerve end en
countering
each change of en
                viron skin

    I   touch thing
    I   touch I in touching
    I   touch thing touching me
    touching

The finger forefinger on either hand
                        makes a direction
            hesitates   on the air
            stabs   with diffidence
            once   twice   once
            & curls finger curls
            round   (that & the next finger

                thing

                    when
                    comes
                    thru the air   slowly
                    diffidently   certainly
                    the other (either fore
                                    finger to
                    touch curl round   ex

                change.

Where were we, Descartes?

p   r   e   c   i   s   e

Let us start with the finger

Omens

rose &
The wood-pigeon /   fell

small boys flew comets
in the park

a blue-veined rose

thursday — thursday
delivered of a baby &

again
        delivered of
                a baby
from the womb of living
to the life of night

9 months from her birth to her weaning
                gate to her berth
9 months of imperfect breathing
I her mother labouring her death
                heavy breasted cementing
                her cradle in the earth
                made her path straight

another pairing: mother with a lily
framed in the doorway; dear friend with a
                cyanotic rose

the blonde sweet nurse assisting at the birth
the doctor who cut the cord

cordis   ;   corda

afterward: the hallowed days
                          scoured by God.

for Bill & Marion

The flowers swell & swell at me
across the hospital room
across
greased lino
swell
yellow & blue;
next
a brown paper rubbish
bag
a white striped
towel a
stainless steel
sink in
fluorescent light
fluoresce
yellow chrysanthemums
yellow carnations
the yellow lobes of
irises
that are altogether
blue
& keep saying it:
their silence is inexhaustible —
this kind of conversation
I have never quite had with you, my friends
before
(the leaves are very cool and dark & smell good)
             yellow, yellow
                  & blue.

'in search of the indigenous'

parked cars, public holiday
a sign up, confusion over money
careful gravel paths, past the
creosote wedding reception to the
tea tables, where a boy in a
wheel chair is fed from a spoon
& what comes from his mouth
has the consistency of mucus white,
upstairs, by gravel walks
on a secluded lawn, to
the thick girl in black slacks
her older escort and
a thin woman white cardigan
shoulders angled to the birds
cross legged,
the peacock performs
his slow dance
beautiful not
ragged & naked of
bars; his brown female
sidelong before him
like
the pianist brilliantined
framing his wife's face
while she turns pages
her looks irrelevant to his
act
arrested by a strong
fragrance I turn & grasp
a peony huge pink &
almost blown
this is not it.
the sweet perfume is
from a common tree,
a pea flower whose yellow
calls across the valley among
azalea rhododendron &
exotica which surround
the RIMU rooted down into
the earth or does it suck

the air, it streams as if
its element is water
& fuses with
the reddest rhododendron.
KOWHAI is also there
far up misted under with
forget me not.
cherry, looks ordinary
& shy
a lilac creepers flower
lends ambi-
guity to the air, close it
details nightshade or
potato flower
but mauve.
I
climb upward
to escape the gardens
trickery & find
almost solace in
hawthorn pink & white
leaning together, rankness
of elder, long grass a few
sheep but up against
cleft Cargill new houses
are too tall, built for the
view only.
I descend
passing the charming pink adobe
its air of neglect, its varnished door
thru the adventure playground
& past the doves
fly —
seagulls/TARAAPUNGA
to the harbour mouth.

Fiona Farrell Poole

Charts to shores rarely visited

Tracks — bird/beast/angel?
Old fires.
Soft imprint of buttocks in the sand
food talk and sleeping
all dust.
Twigs point towards the desert.

*

All roads lead to other roads.
Every arrival a departure.
We swoop to the centre. Drive through the frame.
Tracks converge on a narrow hill
gorse and thistle in the gullies.
Light butters the tops.

*

6 feet is all a man needs.
He can spread his arms
just so far.
Pinned to the board.

*

Strange how loudly paint
can whoop and yell.
How it can hiss and
slide.

*

Maps.
'This way to MMM's house'
'The Enchanted Wood'
'Derwent Water'
These lead inward.
Follow the arrows down the gut
past billowed night through
soft restraining flaps press
release and fall to
colour curled tight in a corner.

Jigsaw

In a corner of their bedroom
under dust they
keep their jigsaw.

On wet evenings they
reassemble the patterns
of summer.

Trees and the smell of mushrooms
twigs in her mouth
sweating grass
spotted sheets
babies and cats and a red carpet
a bay and the wipers going
one   two
one   two.

But she keeps some pieces
tucked among her hankies

and he has a bit of the sky
locked away
in a small drawer.

Resolution Bay

*'He took hold of the flesh of his own Arm
with his Teeth and made signs of eating . . .'*
                              Cook's Journal

The fish in these bays remember us.
They have sucked blood.
Rocks ran with fluids.
And once
a basket leaned against this tree,
flax bent to bursting.

Morning.
You invite the fish under the cliff
to death by eating
unwisely.
('Every squid a barbed one.')

————

You got me jumping.
You got me filled.
You got me fluid.
Let's go fishing.
Go on. Take out
your hook.

Your soft hook.

————

I am floating near the cliff.
No sound.
Rocks.
Trees.
Shadows hold me
60 feet above ground.
The cliff is weathering.
Winter, summer.
I can lay a finger in the ridges
on your face.
Cup my hands in the crevice
at your neck.
Curl in the crack
you open to me.

————

With love to your shoes
with love to your tee shirt
with love to your wet hair
with love to the scratch on your finger.

A different circle opens and closes here.
Temporary
like a fish's mouth.
Silver in first light.
Grey by evening.

Feast for one day.

Cemetery, Oamaru

April.
Leaves crack and shatter.
Periwinkle binds
a snare for living feet.

Angels.
We used to called them fairies.
Chalk white.
Up from the slab
in one night.

———

It's a family business.
'Those early ones
were laid in pine.
Draped in swansdown.
Embroidered with pansies,'
the undertaker tells me.
'And over there
by the macrocarpa
they fell on stones.
They're still whole.'

But the fruitflies know better.
They hang about.

———

Did the trump sound?
And were we too busy in the
garden to hear?
Earth cracks
and in the crevices
hands tear at wrappings.
The party's over.

Save the paper.
Keep the string.
The cards in the top drawer.

———

We built huts in the long grass.
We had a fort in the macrocarpa.
This is where Graham fell off his bike.
And this is where we tickled Neil's penis
till it stood up,
pink as a birthday candle.
Hawthorn and brown grass and
pale flowers in glass
centrepiece to the feast.
Then we burst the bubble
and we crawled through the iron gate
onto the slab.

Warm as flies.

Three births

Clot
phlegm
pearl of my body.

Snag
knot in the red skein.

Paper flower
spreading in water.

Tadpole
lizard
curled snug in the cranny.

Cling
unblinking
then slip into the sun
Susannah.

———

It's the eating of babies
that draws my attention.

First, the umbilicus
a neat snap jaguar
tug quick swallow
like a hen twisting
seeds in her crop.

Next, the afterbirth
jellies of conception
the lickings of cream
whipped thick across
her shoulders.

Her body
round as marshmallows
sweet-scented
her legs buttocks stomach
smooth as custard.

———

Then there was the one that got away.
Wriggled and sank in the dark water.

The doctor said 'If it comes when
you're at home just pop it in a
bottle. I'd like to have a look.'

Pop you in a bottle?

My black olive?

My son?

Moving

My father, white as an onion, drops
heavy into earth hands
clamped to Christ.

Poppies dribble from old men.
They file towards the cannon on the hill
skirting the hole.

This time.

———

'Cry for your kitten. Why don't you?'
he said. 'Cry'.

But I dug my spoon in swallowed
every bit cornflake furball swelling.

Tears — they're easy.
For damp aunts and Bambi's mother.
This pain is bulbous. It shoots
suddenly. Bud and branch.

Your throat hurts.

———

The place is a mess and
nothing is where it used to be.
Muddle and scatter.
And this fantail (poppy-bright

brisk as an angel) swings in
the door. For a minute
death flirts in my kitchen.
On my cupboard. My curtains.
Death trills
that's it
that's it.

I crouch on an applebox cry
for Dad and an icecream
from the shop and a
comic to make it better.

But the place is a mess and
nothing is where is used to be.

She dies and I write her letters

Palmerston North
August 1982

Reports differ.
Perhaps one morning
(you planned coffee
at ten the cat
by the stove)
your body rioted.
No fuss no pain
a soft invasion
ambushed by thousands
in the takeover bid.
You ate a biscuit
read the paper
heard no explosion
no colonists
racing through blood.
(You washed a plate

fed the cat.)
Observers reported
No Change.
Life as Normal.

And one night you find a
fist raised under the skin.

October 1982

I've been weeding
cocksfoot eyebright
jumbling and shoving
a stroppy lot (as
for those docks we
all know about them
and their strikes . . .)

And you're back.
Head like a dandelion.

You can't keep a
good weed down . . .

Cambridge
England
Guy Fawkes Day 1983

Just for the record
it's autumn here
on the sixth circle.
Fire and smoke
sparks in dark trees
and screams from
the big wheel
the dipper
the space ride.
And just for the record
you, my dear, are

watching spring
from the further rim
tucked in a tangle
of books and blanket.
Flowers flare
inches from your window
and (just for the record)
a bird sings.
I think of your
soft bedded hump and
coffee by your heater
your shoulders breasts
shaking with the fun of us
and all those words we've
tossed at one another

just for the record.

January 1984

I want to gulp you down
like the old god my
body's loose and old
bag it'll hold us both
(you and any army).
Come spring and warm
weather pop there you'd
be shiny pink ready
to go again . . .

May 1984

You are thin to begin
such a journey
and the weather is bad.
If you were my pony
I'd hold you back.
You need rest
and feeding

your coat fallen
your white body
bald as a berry
my darling.
But you toss your head
catch the rhythm
step it out
so sure.
One reads of such partings.
There is always one
shrinking to nothing
on the skyline.
There is always one
left waving
squinting into the sun.

The old house burns

Sleeping at my grandmother's
was being on a ship
outside my window pine trees
pennants flying on the wind
booming up the gully we
stormed towards the mountains.
(GentleJesusifIshoulddie
I prayed with fervour under white cover.)

———

The gully pines smoulder
puddles bubble and
the chookhouse flares.
Hop, little flame, hop.
Kiss fruit.
Kiss flower.
Run to tree.
Snap twig.
Twitter.
See green

See red.
See black.

———

Flames sneak through curtains finger
white beds tiptoe to the kitchen peel
open cupboards strip walls to bone.
Nothing left but the soft black sponge
which used to be the telephone.

———

The print burns.
The groom leers
boils burst on
sheer wedding cheeks
babies' legs
twist to ash.
This house stood sepia
behind so many backs.
These roses cornered aunts and cousins.
Grandad with Tip on the verandah.
Fat girl (my mother) on a pony.
The uncle who went mad
in curls.

Night interior

The house creaks and clicks its teeth.
Children huddle under leaves
hoping for pebbles in the morning
and no birds trusting in gingerbread
forgetful of ovens. Twigs/bones/
fingers clutch and curl.

I sit by the heater.
Rain presses leaf
by leaf.
Bread baking.

Night scales the fence.

Keri Hulme

Moeraki Conversations 2

He Wahi Tapu

Shell knife
'You digging another hole for the dunny?'
Yeah, breathing hard and stabbing the earth
on the safe fringes
sand and more sand and shovel and aching
and suddenly soot
calcined shells and broken fishjaws browned
by hundred on hundred still years
underground, and on the iron edge
a flake of flint chipped in deliberate small notches
long as my finger. Don't touch!
'Hey it's sharp!'
        grinning at my white eyes
        grinning and carving the air
        hoping for blood beads
        'Tu! Tu! Tu!'
shrill above the sea
'E, who taught you that?'

            'Nobody . . . "

Moeraki Conversations 4

(dream fragment, Seaweed Hair Climbing)
There is a great height either side and
the rocks are revealed momentarily in
the gulf below when the sea washes
out
but the first thing is the air
clinging to it like a kutu on a head
black hair, not shiny, with a slightly
rusty tinge,
not slippery but it *was* growing from
a cliff

crawling along, looking down —
danger! 'ware rocks hard rocks!
Come along! says someone higher
then a hank of clump of hair comes
out in my hand and falls down the
slope, only a little way but have to
leave it behind the rocks the height
are too much
but the feeling that something very
precious has been forsaken —
Getting up shivering in the night,
wrapping myself in the canvas-backed
blanket like it's a cloak and pakehas
haven't been invented, going outside to
watch for shooting stars or the greenghost
flicker of wildfire that is never where my
eyes expect it, or anything.

E tangi ana moana . . .

Coming inside in the dawnlight, I see our
keyhole is plugged with cobwebs.

Moeraki Conversations 6

They have lit this year's fire on the
beach and it has exploded in flowers
of flame and sparks vivid against the
night.
We are full of New Year paua and
chicken and whisky and new potatoes
and salad and crayfish and beer. We
are full of talk and singing, sprawled
in a ring round the fire, telling each
other what has happened to us during
this dying year, what we hope for in
the time to come.
I can feel the old ones crowd round,
intent on our laughter and songs,
beaming at reunion.

We join hands, an unbroken circle at
midnight.
And then one by one, two by two, we
drift away to bed.

I watch the fire till it has nearly died,
logs eaten to ashes, white and grey
and yellow on the dullred ember bed.

'Come to the funeral rites of the fire —
Orion leans towards morning

There is only us

me wrapped in some dead soldier's jacket
drinking the end of a year I never expected to see

white waves lapping
the island hunched in shadow

a new net full of holes am I
waiting in the dark
waiting in the dark

Smile; we will go on
listening to the waves
watching for the dawning

calling a long farewell to friends
gone into the great night

falling asleep in the sun
on this new morning —

      'E hoa ma
      haere, haere, haere ra ki te po
      Ka noho mai au ki Moeraki
      i te ao marama

Pa mai tō reo aroha

Seaweed floats in a brown tangled rack, a
tack out from the rocks.
It falls and rise, breathing with the water.

On the beach, the apricot and gold gravel
turns rusty orange at wave-edge.
There is a long streak of irondark sand
where Matuatiki runs out to the sea.
There are shattered black rocks round all
the arc of bay.

The cliffs are made of claystone, greenish
and ochre, with odd intrusions of pink
melted rocks. The thornbushes along the
tops slant away from the sea. They are
shaved and trimmed and wounded by the
wind.

At each end of the kaik' bay the cliff goes
down in humps to stand blunt-nosed
against the sea. But the rocks creep further
out, black arms, reefs. They are full of
secret pools. The unblinking eyes of octopi
at night.

Today, a cloud of midges weaves and
dances through the evening sun.
There are mysterious glassy tracks on the
sea.
Thin waves hush in, pause, slide away.
Moeraki, calm as untroubled sleep . . .

At night, the penguins bray under the
cribs,
Sometimes the old ghosts from
Kihipuku steal in, for warmth and
company.
The dog will prick his ears and growl,
the cat snarl a little, then both sigh
and stretch and settle again.

We eat and talk and read until the
lamps flicker. Then we go to sleep in
the narrow cupboard bunks, and the
sea has all our dreams.
Every morning the shags stretch their
necks and slip off Maukiekie. Every
evening they return in a wavering
line.
Sometimes we have seen the living
black wheels of caa'ing whales out in
the woman sea.
Once I found an earwig big as my
thumb in the cliffs, moulding her
body round her pale brood.
When the seaweed is thick onshore,
the kelp-flies swarm in their
thousands, pattering like rain against
the lighted windows.
On another day, the sea smashes in
against twin-armed Tikoraki. The
blowhole booms.
The elephant-black rocks rumble back and
forward in a murderous herd.
The air is thick and salt and full of
roaring. Great waves, crests streaming
back in long white drifts, explode against
the little island. Maukiekie, kia
manawanui!
Yellow foam scums the beach. Rain drives
down, and Matuatiki swells, carving
curving braids in the sand.
Further south, out of the reach of the reef,
the rocks Tutimakohu and Te Karipi stand
on tiptoe, each suffocating pillar dreading
hightide in this lash and swirl of storm-
driven sea.
I crouch against the claystone, like a child
huddling close to its mother.
I watch the waves wage their long war
against the land, the land her long
resistance.

Wine Song [23]

e hine
there is a name I use in the daytime
and a name I use at night,
names for walking on the leftside,
names for treading on the right —
                    pass the bottle, lady
I have a name for walking the tideline,
another for swimming in the sea,
and one for when I'm landbound
and several when flying free —
                    observe the level of the wine
I have a name I am called in my living
and a secret one waiting for death,
the first for all breaths I am breathing,
the last one for the last breath —
                    time flows slowly, lady
O names from friends and lovers,
names from enemies
names in war and fighting
and names in peace —
one name still before me,
another to leave behind,
and not one name fits all me,
not one name I can find . . .
                    Pass the bottle, lady,
                    observe the level of the wine—
                    time flows slowly, lady,
                    all down the line
and what name would you give me?

Mushrooms and Other Bounty

[Te Kaihau —2]

Picking mushrooms, grumbling over their pale heads
heavy and sodden-gilled from continuing rain

Still, they are chance-fruit
like naked frostfish found on bitter glittering mornings

the jewels of phrases I have been given
tossed away by careless strangers

and the real people who slid in from the black
at the back of my dreams, and played,
until I imprisoned them in words

Chance-fruit: what past bones
tuned my ears to catch the inner chant
of shining-cuckoo song?

And once, walking a sea-line yet again,
I caught the only whitebait of that tide
stranded by a sandbank in an errant finger of water
already cooked by the sun.

He Hōhā

> Bones tuned, the body sings—

See me,
I am wide with swimmer's muscle, and a bulk and
    luggage I carry curdled on hips;
I am as fat-rich as a titi-chick, ready for the far ocean
    flight.

See me,
I have skilled fingers with minimal scars, broad feet that
    caress beaches,
ears that catch the music of ghosts, eyes that see the
    landlight, a pristine womb
untouched, except by years of bleeding, a tame unsteady
    heart.

See me,
I am a swamp, a boozy drain with stinking breath, a
    sour sweetened flesh;
I am riddled with kidneyrot, brainburn, torn gut,
    liverfat, scaled with wrinkles,
day by day I am leached, even between smiles, of that
    strange water, electricity.

See me,
I am my earth's child,

> and she, humming
> considers her cuts and scars, and debates our
>   death.
> Mean the land's breast, hard her spine when
>   turned against you;
> jade her heart.

Picture me a long way from here —
back bush, a rainbird calling,
the sea knocking shore.

It is cliché that once a month, the moon stalks through
    my body,
rendering me frail and still more susceptible to brain
    spin;
it is truth that cramp and clot and tender breast beset —
    but then
it is the tide of potency, another chance to walk through
    the crack between worlds.

What shall I do when I dry, when there is no more
    turning with the circling moon?
Ah suck tears from the wind, close the world's eye;
Papatuanuku still hums.

But picture me a long way from here.

Waves tuned, the mind-deep sings

> She forgot self in the city, in the flats full of dust
>   and spiderkibbled flies;
> she forgot the sweetness of silence in the rush and
>   roar of metal nights;
> no song fitted her until she discovered her kin, all
>   swimmers in the heavy air of sea;
>
> she had lost the supple molten words, the rolling
>   thunder,
> the night hush of her mother's tongue;

she had lost the way home, the bright road, the
    trodden beach, the mewling gulls,
the lean grey toe of land.

In the lottery of dreams, she gained prize of a
    nightmare, a singular dark.

But picture her a long way from there,
growing quiet until she heard herself whispered
    by the sea on the blackest night,
and echoed in the birds of morning.

Keening, crooning, the untuned spirit —
I am a map of Orion scattered in moles across this
  firmament of body;
I am the black hole, the den where katipo are busy
  spinning deadhavens,
and he won't go, the cuckoo child.
Jolted by the sudden thud and shatter, I have gone
  outside to find
the bird too ruffled, too quiet, the barred breast broken,
  an end of the far travelling.

Tutara-kauika, you father of whales, you servant
    of Tangaroa,
your little rolling eye espies the far traveller —
    quick!
whistle to him, distract, send him back to the
    other island;
I don't mind ever-winter if summer's harbinger is
    so damaged, damaging.

He turned full to face me, with a cry to come home —
do you know the language of silence, can you read
  eyes?

When I think of my other bones, I bleed inside,
and he won't go, the cuckoo-child.

It is not born; it is not live; it is not dead;
it haunts all my singing, lingers greyly, hates and hurts

and hopes impossible things.
And Papatuanuku is beginning her ngeri, her anger is
    growing, thrumming in quakes and tsunami,
and he won't go, the cuckoo's child.

    O, picture me a long way from here;
    tune the bones, the body sings;
    quiet the mind, the spirit hums,
    and Papatuanuku trembles, sighs;
    till then among the blood and dark
    the shining cuckoo spreads his wings
    and flies this hōhā, this buzz and fright,
    this wave and sweat and flood,
    this life.

Vivienne Joseph

Work of Fiction

today, when birds & flowers rise
bubbling to the spring's surface

I join the lunchtime strollers
(my daughter's dog beside me)

& a man in overalls pauses to pat
the small, white animal & talk

& all the while he's looking at me
— this could be Chekhov's tale . . .

he wants to know if I'm unattached
I look down at the dog on the lead

discover a literary device —
myself, talking to a stranger

Stillbirth

That time (in ignorance) I held the pig
he smiled at my efforts to keep it still
then plunged his knife
                              (he'd kept it hidden)
deep into its jugular vein
& it screamed — on & on
as I covered my ears the rain splattered
when I looked, I saw blood.

The only other time I've seen such blood
— such a blossoming
was when my child was born — too soon
& I in shock became once again
                    that sixteen-year-old girl
watching a dying animal
          & the man who stood over it
                    smiling, wiping his knife.

Sex Films

I go to school with my daughters, wearing a dress
(not jeans please)
they giggle in the front row — I, with a sudden
preference for darkness
sit at the back, remember books my mother gave me
to be read
then tossed up in the wardrobe with
decapitated dolls
stamp album
shoe-box nest of sparrows' eggs
we blew life out needle-holes
as bubbles through a pipe
the teacher puts the film on backwards
everyone laughs
the priest loudest
(then he departs)
Later, their eyes night-huge
wasn't the girl pretty
didya see the flowers
& that cute baby
the outside air tastes good
as we walk I hold them close
Next day, under a hanging sky
we see a dog
running on leaden footpaths
his masculinity unsheathed
screaming red
the background suburban grey
& not a flower in sight.

Heredity

My daughter's seen Macbeth
says it was okay & thanks
to Polanski's taste in naked
crones & blood-spurts
the boys were kept entertained

She says she's more into Romeo
though it could do with a re-write
                              & smiles
I don't tell her I know
                    what she means
she's three on a string at the moment
one for conversation
                one because he looks good
the third's got a panel-van
I listen, take it all in
                hoping it's not too late
to inherit some of this
                    from my children . . .

In Retrospect

last night we met for the first time
    this morning after rain
                              a thrush
    the clouds lifting
& left of centre-stage, the sun
                    making its entrance
& if there seems to be
                a certain clarity of light
                a breathlessness in the air
& if my heart (that overworked pump)
                    beats erratically
                    — it's irrelevant

let's keep this thing
                    in perspective

Those Horses . . .

'The days run away like wild horses
over the hills' (Charles Bukowski)

Here, old-lady willows, their garments threadbare
drop copious tears   the river
now swollen, brown & wandering from its banks
has gouged two sockets deeply in my lawn
I fear the glaucous stare
              — that darkness the rain has released
& I'm trying to write you a letter
but the ink & summer are running away fast
& the paper cannot hold the weight of my words
nothing is as it should be
                              nothing is permanent
I write letters which are full of rain
& you listen for the hoofbeats of those horses . . .

In the Camp of the Chameleon

When the horse-drawn caravan arrives in town,
it attracts people like children to a video game.

My wife sings, 'I wish I lived in a caravan. . .'
I say 'Didn't your mother ever tell you, you
never should, play with the gypsies. . .'

'He calls to the stars,' she says, 'And they come
to him. He gentles them in his hands. . . strokes
the finer points. . .'
'He's an astrologer?' I ask.
'Maybe,' she says, as she unbuttons her blouse.
'Maybe not,' she calls, as she lifts up her skirts,
runs out of the house.

Nights I'm alone, he isn't.

Whistling, I go in search of the rover — down
through the valley so shady.
He's waiting for me. Has painted his face.
The colours stand up and are accountable: Red,
Gold and Green.

I show him my gun. The Knight of Swords takes it away
The fire dreams. My wife dances barefoot.
He tells stories and the birds come down out of the
trees. . . He plays his fiddle. The note is for me.
I read it and believe.

In the morning when I awake, I'm alone,
holding the tail of a lizard
                    and it moves. . .

Framed

Turn out the light
                         open the door
put the chair
               in the middle of the room
a street lamp shines
                  through the window
illuminates the space
                 you must watch
this space must be watched
                 at all times
for further enlightenment
                    listen
to the footsteps
            have they stopped?
they have stopped
            there are two guns
one fires
          one shot only is fired

Jan Kemp

For R. A. K. Mason

I came unasked to your funeral;
the solemn men, dark-coated,
your friends, give you their pass
to heaven by a natural door:
we were to have lauded you,
you died a week too soon.

From where I stand on the edge
I hear your words they read —
through the windows of the chapel,
I see cabbage tree flax, flat & flex,
licking the blue sky,
a whip in a green wind.

Poem

It was your face.
It was shy.
We walked.
It was your head.
It was lit with sun.
I unbuckled your belt.
Hush, don't speak,
the yellow flowers are bursting.

Poem

A puriri moth's wing
lies light in my hand —

my breath can lift it

light as this torn wing
we lie on love's breath.

White Dawn

Last night you traced
my veins & made me whole —

sang the song of songs
at your fingertips on my flesh.

I look at freesias
& at the sun.

The touch is rare
the breath undone.

Timing

Timing
timing
the timing must be right —
the first flush must come
like a spasm of spring after snow
when of a sudden
recognition
that this is the green moment
the heart of grass kicks
beneath burying crystals

in the heat of a second
the shocked snow
melts to a blush
green blades
dangerous as death
dangerous as life
green blades

shoot for the sun.

Down the First Road

Down the first road I ever walked,
all the boys
at the coffee stalls cried out:
hi Fatimah, good journey Fatimah,
as if they knew —
                    it must have
shone out of my instep,
the swing of my blue dress
like morning spilt on shadows,

I was flowered a thousand times over.

But there was more than this walking,
flame leaves leaping
off my skin, my feet dancing:
I was a doe
alert & vanishing
                    through tangled caverns
to a clear lake, where I knelt
& drank at your side
the water of light.

At Telegraph Bay

Something in the air I must explore:
a summer day come in winter
dazzling the mica out of these rocks
making the cold sea delicious,
the craggy islands demure in the mist.

A hydrofoil across Telegraph Bay
shirrs up the waves, the sun
brings my skin out of my clothes,
the sea from under this hat
catches at my eye reflecting and reflecting
off a blue cloth sewn with tiny mirrors.

Junks

I should like it
if the Chinese ancestors
lying here in their bones
in the rubble of a grey-green gully
would let me take down their messages;

I could fashion them
into tiny paper junks
and breathe their sails full
and free them
to the movement of the sea.

Turkey Talk

Now that you've been chosen from the rest,
frozen and netted in red plastic
your bilingual tag denoting name and poundage,
CANADA GRADE A stencilled on your breast,
you, self-basting boasting bird, and I
must come to terms.
                    Your hours are short
                    my time is rushed.

Your pale stippled poor plucked skin
is no match for my resources, hot running water,
these two strong hands and an iron will,
though you're solid, I'll admit, and secretive;
your neck is locked within your breast,
old ostrich, your giblets in your ass —
these treasures I seek.
But what of your ruddy wattle, garbled gobbledegook,
what of your history — where are these?
your Mexican ancestors carted as bullion to Europe
returned with settlers to the eastern States —
countless harvests you've known, untold ears of corn.

But now, by some fluke of fate, you're in my clutches,
now that I've forced you open, rinsed you out,
now that I've stitched your skin over cavities

stuffed with herbs, onions, celery, crumbs;
now that you're garlanded with buttered cheesecloth,
your plump legs (crossed reverently, before the fire)
all trussed up to the pope's nose,

let me invite you
(for I'm sure you'll survive the burning)
let me invite you to be the golden guest of honour
at our table, just four hours from now;
you'll drip with your own juices
be fêted with all the frills of a sacrifice
then we'll consume you bird, oh yes, you'll tenderly be eaten.

Thanksgiving '76

A New World: Homage to Wallace Stevens
for Pauli

"Without a doubt, life loses its charms of make-
believe painlessly" HELMUT BONIFACE FANTASTICO

I saw you amber gentle dreaming
over deep green land

and as you waken
from darkling moon   soil
and forest eyes
to dance upon the shore
fresh as light
spills on morning beach

      perhaps I see him too
      running the fall of ocean water   sand
      between his thighs
      noticing
      how golden and how blue
      the scents commingle

how the daytime wafer moon
above the headland
is quick with light —

how the sun
melodic from lip to cup
makes wine of this.

Cilla McQueen

Timepiece

I got home from work and looked at
my watch, and it said
Ten to five, so I did the washing and
picked some greens and tidied up the
kitchen, and sat down and had a cup of coffee,
and looked at my watch and still it said
Ten to five, so I did some ironing and
made the beds and thought Hell I might
get all the housework done in one day
for a change, then looked at my watch
but nope, no change, and I turned on the
radio and it said Ten to five, so
I cleaned the bathroom like mad and
picked some flowers and wrote some
letters and some cheques and scrubbed
the kitchen floor and got started on the
windows — by this time I was getting a bit
desperate I can tell you, I was thinking
alternately Yay! soon there'll be no more to
do and I'll be free, and Jeez what if I
RUN OUT? I did in fact run out, and out,
and out, past the church clock saying
Ten to five and the cat on the corner with
big green eyes ticking away, and up into the
sky past the telephone wires, and
up into the blue, watchless, matchless, timeless
cloud-curtains, where I hide, and
it is silent, silent.

By the water

Dark glissades to meet the
light   on reefs of air: I find you
dismembered in the landscape
among indolent hills
                    You disperse & are

gone again
            I slice with quick knuckle & twist
of hand, pluck with finger & thumb light
skin from the dark
hill's blade; place
                    palm down flat on
liquid light, curl fingers & ripple up
wry tangled faces

oh but
            I am strung so blind under this
twilight sky
                I give up focus, there is only
salt-lick on nape of hill   to say how I
fit you, how you keep
arriving under
                my hands, simple as water.

No Poem

I like the relationship between thought & paper
to get faster   & a good way to practise is writing
down everything as it comes out   simplification
comes later with organisational experience   the work
of fining down
                the more you play around with words
the more they frighten you with the punch they
pack   like the images I cover my walls with
which as a result of the distortion caused by tearing
out by the roots have become unfixed scraps of reality
exploding on contact
                    which is why we seem to be picking
our way through a minefield just a few of us anarchists
white flags & mortars both ways across no mans land

Rock Poem, Carey's Bay

At a quarter past three on a sunny
Wednesday afternoon in a niche

in the big rock above the bay
ladying it over the houses

I have established a line between my
right eye & the tip of Taiaroa Head.

Hills swing half circle either side
& the landscape is caged by power lines

constellations of thistles drifting
across. As the tide goes out

the land is very slowly rising to
uncover blue veined acres of sand.

At a distance of infinity there is
little trouble with focus. Its when

you really come up against things
that you get problems with vision.

You can get so close in through the
distorted cages of parallax that what

youre looking at is invisible. Nose
squashed frog eyes fingertips white

what then? A moment of disorientation
& you pass through like Alice

gradually beginning to see clearly?
Sometimes it seems that what youre up

against is simple cruelty of mirrors.
Yet there are times & places such as

on this lichen covered relic in the sun
above the sea & Aramoana that I discover

both space & an anchor to the earth,
an invisible grid of reliable perspective

amid an expanding universe of
thistledown. Times like these I call it

balancing at the interface, tiptoe on
a point between the world & dream.

Homing in

Here again.
Darks falling. Stand
on the corner of the verandah
in the glass cold clear
night, looking out
to emerald & ruby harbour
lights:
        too sharp to stay
out long,
            enough just to
greet the bones lying
on the moon
& two fishing boats
homing in.

Living Here

Well you have to remember this place
is just one big city with 3 million people with
a little flock of sheep each so we're all sort of
shepherds
            little human centres each within an outer
circle of sheep around us like a ring of
covered wagons   we all know we'll probably
be safe when the Indians finally come

down from the hills   (comfortable to live
in the Safest Place in the World)
                              sheep being
very thick & made of wool & leather
being a very effective shield as ancient
soldiers would agree.
                      And you can also
sit on them of course & wear them & eat them
so after all we are lucky to have these
sheep in abundance   they might
have been hedgehogs — Then we'd all be
used to hedgehogs & clothed in prickles
rather than fluff
                      & the little sheep would
come out sometimes at night under the moon
& we'd leave them saucers of milk
                                  & feel sad
seeing them squashed on the road
Well anyway here we are with all this
cushioning in the biggest city in the world
its suburbs strung out in a long line
& the civic centre at the bottom of
Cook Strait   some of them Hill Suburbs
& some Flat Suburbs & some more prosperous
than others
              some with a climate that embarrasses
them & a tendency to grow strange small fruit
some temperate & leafy   whose hot streets lull

So here we are again in the biggest
safest city in the world   all strung out
over 1500 miles one way   & a little bit
the other
              each in his woolly protection
so sometimes it's difficult to see out
the eyes   let alone call to each other
which is the reason for the loneliness some
of us feel
              and for our particular relations
with the landscape   that we trample
or stroke with our toes or eat or lick

tenderly or pull apart
                    and love   like an
old familiar lover who fits us
curve to curve   and hate because it
knows us & knows our weakness
We're calling fiercely to each other
through the muffled spaces   grateful for
any wrist-brush
                    cut of mind or touch of music,
lightning in the intimate weather of the soul.

Low Tide, Aramoana

Sky with blurred pebbles
a ruffle on water

sky with long stripes
straight lines of ripples

sky-mirror full of
sand and long pools

I step into the sky
the clouds shiver and disappear.

thin waterskin over underfoot cockles here & there old timber
& iron orange & purple barnacled crab shells snails green
karengo small holes

I look up from walking at
a shy grey heron on
the point of flight.

oystercatchers whistle stilts & big gulls eye my quiet
stepping over shells & seaweed towards the biggest farthest
cockles out by the channel beacon at dead low tide

It's still going out.
I tell by the moving

of fine weeds in
underwater breeze.

takes a time to gather these rust & barnacle coloured whole
sweet mouthfuls

Low.
and
there's a sudden

wait

            .

for the moment
of precise
solstice: the whole şea
                hills and sky
                wait

                .

                and everything
                stops.

high gulls hang seaweed is arrested the water's skin
tightens we all stand still. even the wind evaporates
leaving a scent of salt

                .

I snap out start back get moving before the new tide back
over cockle beds through clouds underfoot laying creamy
furrows over furrowed sand over flats arched above & below
with blue & yellow & green reflection & countered reflection

                .

                look back to
                ripples
                begun again.

Vegetable Garden Poem II

Silver beet stalks glow white
neon tubes. The sun goes in to them
and shines back off the dark leaves.
Clouds come over the Potters'
roof travelling fast scored by the
cabbage trees. The telegraph poles
have remained alive. They have
branches and shiny brown knobs that
hold wires and pass them across.
The power lines are straight and
curved, parallel crisscrossing and
converging. The poles are anchors
to the ground and vectors out of
the earth.

Looking down, the vegetable garden's
chocolate brown and green. I'm
down here beside the silver beet between
two thistles. There is a very old and
rusty iron drum we brought back from
Aramoana lying to my left. The skin
of it is stippled orange indigo and violet.
A starry daisy's shadow polishes it in
coming and going breeze. I turn to face
the plum tree. Red eyes wink in there.

The ash whispers.

Suddenly in a gust we are all swept
sideways hair in a glitter. Now here in
front of me is a corrugated copper red and
green and black hot water tank, elegantly
eroded. A pile of soft orange old bricks,
corrugated iron, docks and blackberry.
Up the hill the big gum tree is the shape
of the clouds travelling east. I strip
a seedhead and let the seeds go flying.
The thistles move slowly their purple
crowns. A slow silent willow dances behind.
The grasses each have their exclusive

seed head design. Whatever it is, the idea
is to get up very tall and slim into the
maximum possible windspace, and start broadcasting.

On the Problem of Remembering Your Face

Old sailors with their
celestial navigation knew
the trick: not to look straight
at, but past, catching
your star deviously
(a delicate business, this,
like remembering a dream)
in the corner of the eye

Continually you elude me;
I'm having trouble with
this obliquity —
there is, for example, this
mouth above my forehead, this
shoulder beyond my cheekbone, a
familiar gesture of yours,
somewhere, only just
out of vision —

Each time, naively, I
forget about the old
sailors and look, directly, to
see you disintegrate in
mocking ripples, then
reassemble gradually your
familiar fragments as a hand, an
eyebrow, a bone beneath the skin
just beyond the corner of
my eye

It is the plight of
Orpheus, who in the
moment of turning sent
his beloved

exploding in splinters
outwards into darkness
— instantly to reassemble
into a perfect image of
herself, always
henceforth
(a dream of a shadow
slipping through fingers)
just beyond his
field of vision —

I could remember you, easily,
if you didn't fly
apart all the
time,
like this

Some Poets

they get
shit on their shoes
& trail it everywhere

their
ragged impossible
tenderness

ah so bloody romantic
still I wish

huh.
fuck wishing.

time for some
naked light!

beauty in spareness.
what is & what is not.

Axis

shells pipe sea music
& fern fronds punch
soft green heads into my palm

within
the tiny ladder of the DNA
the mighty spiral of the Milky Way

living
in circles of time
growing towards the light

Cracks

thousands of tiny
cracks, snaking
forwards & back
& simultaneously neither

like when you can
see the future
becoming, exquisitely.

Nuages

walking along
when a slim sword
of sunlight bars my way

light sensitive bells in doorways

somewhere across space
a bell sounds,
cling clong

Baby

for Pascal Harris

aurora under a
kite of stars

Pascal born
1623

atmospheric
pressure laws

sane balance
of liquids

hydraulic
thinking

souple
clair
et puissant

Learning to Read

I remember the look
of the unreadable page

the difficult jumble

& then the page
became transparent

& then the page
ceased to exist:

at last I was riding this bicycle all by myself!

Interference

Outside it is
slanting green hail in midsummer
the sound of the sea in a shell to your ear
What a performance I mutter

as I climb up the ladder to bring down
Muriel from the top shelf
where I find she is going through
the correspondence, methodically

tearing it to shreds
What a performance I whisper
and settle down again at the typewriter
saying excuse me to Muriel, who agrees

to share the chair grudgingly, although
I can see she is holding her breath and
spreading out as much as possible;
Nevertheless I shoot through to Aramoana

and write a poem on the beach a hundred yards long
on the smooth white sand at
the harbour mouth, walk along
the inside of the channel a little way

until it turns into the sand flats where
the oystercatchers stilts and cockles
shelter from the big waves
rolling in on the seaward side

A smooth green adze, the sea
The haunches of Taiaroa
rise up from its jaw on the water
and rest upon soft green paws; I hear

a loud miaow, and there
is Muriel on the windowsill
staring at me, so I go to the door
and open it on to the shining path

and purple cineraria, but she has changed
her mind: she looks at me across
the glass as if I'm mad
A blackbird rips a zigzag through the rain

that is beginning again as I go
back to the desk when Muriel walks in
the other door, hustles me out to the kitchen
and glares at the fridge

What a performance I'm raving away to myself
on the way back to my room again when
Andrea pokes her head out of the shower
and yells Why? What have I done?

So I have to say, huh, sorry darling,
just reciting a bit of a poem
and thinking hell now I really have
flipped, I was talking to myself

From *Four Sonnets*

i

Winter's a finger under the wool, spreading
capillaries of shivers: my boots go gong on
the pavement,
                    I bow to the hungry letterboxes
past Joe's goat & the ship in the bottle in
the window & the kids repairing the old car
all colours & bits & pieces & rust colours
in the corrugated iron fence & the hulls of
ships, gulls wheeling slow
                    & the innkeeper's
daughter down by the water feeding the ducks,
her long striped hair clean as flax:
                    delicate,
the way she divides the bread   And here we
are at the pub, Mungo singing Whistle wind oh
Whistle window Whistle me
                    Oh a ship so tall
but he's too drunk to go fishing today

Janet Charman

do you know what's best for me

i remember
on afternoon
shift
how i stroked
my own passion
into some old lady's
unsunned
flabby back
concentrating
in the afterdinner
hotwash
on stupefying
the sick old body
into fragile
comfort
with these gentle
insistent
attentions

Dettol

Dettoller

je   Dettol
tu   Dettol
elle. Dettol

nous Dettolons
vous Dettolez
elles Dettolent

Comprenez?
oui
Oui quoi?
oui ma soeur   je comprend

je comprend tout à fait

obeying breakfast

we put the sixth slice
in marmalade rind
thick as lips
doltish
banging the china pot
bittersweet hot tea
up the table
stronger than we're used to
ducking the giggle to the plate
outrage
heard fell out of bed
sluice in flood
that bitch Sonia
I blame the daystaff
i thought
that someone
had told her

daring oblivion
doing and undoing
the eight hour shift
before the sisters' table
where Matron sits
in holy isolation
cutting her crust
sly fatigue
keep it down girls

two deaths in one night

in each side room
a body
dropped in the sheets
after long pain
and a look of tense
hectic
between breath
fright

we were going to a rugby party
after work
that night

how we washed their bodies

i took down the cotside
and cut away
the drip
old dressings
and the oxygen mask

Jean said
i'll wash
you hold

     i held
     the dull blank weight
          against warm   me

    his unknown soldier chin
    propped up finally
    and we found a bit of carnation
    to stick between
    his tied together hands

       this was just
       the first one
across the hall
we started on   the other

    how we washed his body

    had to laugh
    in the low light of
    sisters
    office

sipping tea
waiting for the orderlies

to load their long white parcels away
on cold trolleys

      All that shit
      I dont know how you girls can
      Do it
           says the lock forward
brushing his finger into what he hopes is my breast

      Come down the beach with us —
      we went
      two deaths in one night

paranoia

med students
(girl doctors
dont seem so remote
across the candlelight
then in the smoke
he hands me
i see the cunning
little roach clip
is
an artery forcep
no
nurse
goes off
duty
till
the instrument count
is right

there's a lot of heavy lifting looking after wimmin

she sent me
with the bowl
of chopped up bread

in milk
to Nana

here Mum made this
will she really
eat
the disgusting
slops

yes

the old lady
takes the gift
in her fierce
resentful
mouth

tell your mother

oh   never mind

see the garnet ring i wear?
my mother said

i suppose
you can have
this

there are no wombed doctors who'll deliver in the west

pumpkin parasols make their procession
across the lawn
from the compost   to the apricot tree

i phone till the engaged becomes a voice
to be seen at eleven

i bus to the mysterious green door
in The Crescent
i can hear childrens voices in the background

and she puts her fingers inside me
when we've hardly been introduced

one apple on the wire espalier
and behind and before it
the rain drifting
i stir the coldness of the speculum out
with weak tea
and wonder
how the fat rice grains
became suspended
in the wall of the porcelain pot

the woman who wanted to have her cake and eat it

she dreamed she did the splits
waking only with the certainty of her divided body
a toe behind and before
chin up
smiling at the judges

but they don't know she means it

that hair begins under her arms
and she'll allow it
that scant fur starts from her legs
and she lets it spread

at the next performance
they find the beast transformed
her tutu is mid calf
her spartan shoes cross strap upon a field
of velvet ankle

that's up close

but from the gods you only see
a fuzz in the outline of her arabesque

in the patisserie she sips her lemon water
a dancer can't be too careful around fat
this is a bad day

but that night in the show
she curtseyed low
and pressed her face into the armful of red roses
the spotlight belting down around her
and she felt the licking petals
in her bodice
and her bosoms grew
pushing up against the cellophane
towards the scented flowers

till each fell out a full cup overflowed

and then she left the stage
lives at the bach in winter
chops wood
keeps up her dancers muscles
without the injuries

how the woman dealt with her lover
she bathes
she thinks
          'tonight his fingers will sweeten me'
unbuttoning the row of currants on her blouse
tulips
nosing from a plain ground
come on gingerbread man
are you running as fast as you can?

but he's spent today
reclining on a hot tray   and scorched

'Gin and Tonic darling?' she says
and thinks
          'we're just like our parents'

he might not be a dream at all'
that alarms her

well she buckles her stilettos on
thinks that should be slow enough

but there's an upset
he comes puffing up
and overtakes her

and next minute
it's the finish
she bites his head off

Arkles

no view is as good
as my memory of it
back turned
walking the other way
   why is that?

what a lying brain
to believe there are words that convey
exactly
what i can see

as the artist draws
a bowl of fruit
a dozen times

and each globe of seed filled flesh
is rot
by the end of the exercise

who is good enough

to fill
the black avocado skin boots
in the compost?

shit

run down the bay while there's still time
rain's falling
each drop stoppers
into the glass decanter of the ocean
and it all pours back up the beach

walk one way   there's a whole oak
in leaf below the cliff

another   you get the mist subdued
hint
of the volcano

and i looked the bird up later
in a wildlife book
but now i only know it's yellow eyed
drifting the air currents
alive to the flush of inanga
streaking the underside
of the water

and we're the swimmers

i do my backward roll
eyes tight closed
for the moment of vertigo

stand up all wet
good not to have a broken neck
i have another look at Rangitoto
can't see what it's on about yet

Anne French

The solitary life

It's simple. You make coffee, decide
whether to use the white cup
or the glass one, and sit down with a book
of poems — for company merely, like
an animal or a photograph.

Outside a spring day blazes. The fig tree lifts
green hands to the sky, 'Come rain, come breeze,
come sun,' as though winter had lasted years.
There are flowers on the table.
Such richness — coffee, flowers, and silence.

It was not always like this. At seventeen
I lived in a windy house above the bay and battled.
Desire and betrayal washed in and out leaving jetsam
at the high-water mark: jettisoned lovers, old allegiances.
Junk from a wilful and complicated life.

I prefer this. Plenty of time later on for passion,
for the phone-call, the embrace for which nothing
else will do. All you absurd, urgent particularities:
wait there. I'll put you on when the season changes
— next week, perhaps. Or possibly the week after.

All Cretans are liars

Consider the lie as self-reflexive, leading
to an infinite regress. 'Do you do this often?'
sincerely asked is easy to deny
ease being all or most of it, and I
compliant and complicit most easily. One lie
laid to rest then facts resemble bait
and thus were readily taken — picture it,
they say, the Backs, those green lawns, rowing
for your college, the sonorous echo of boys' voices —
i.e. a fly or finger to land a small fish

out of a backwater. That lapse or fault
was simply a failure of imagination. After all
a little water clears us of this act
and the truth is just a small and wrinkled thing.

Collisions

'Of course she's still intransigent,' you said
between bites as though it isn't someone's marriage.
So I took a good thirty seconds to digest it.
'Intransigent nothing.' Sounds as though I was
their counsellor from Marriage Guidance and not
— well, something similar, if less honourable. More
involved. His consolation, her confidante.
A reflex triangle, you might call it, kinked
briefly backwards against gravity.
How much of that you know I daren't assess,
but note the stillness of your eyes, your voice
as we defend them to each other. It's the boys'
team against the girls'. Result: a draw.
We call it off with a point each on the board.

So do you know it all then, or just what he
told you — not quite the same thing — the plot
and some of the dialogue, with a critical commentary
throughout? Not, presumably, how it happened:
the usual collisions of people from a small
country living in a provincial town.
The predictable, in other words, just waiting
for its chance. I was the meat, that's all — he'll
have told you gristle. Or how it ended: dinners
together, celebrations, people left on planes,
assorted fictions stayed intact. Now silence.
It's relief. But forget his elegant phrases, grand
evoked emotion. Let me risk the awkward
truth — it seems (improbably) I loved them both.

Night flying

1: South

Behind and below the wing Motunui shines
an unnatural orange glow between
the curve of mountain the steep
parabola of coast. And you
are down there in those dark fields
in that smudgy town. She has gone
and it is as though she is still
with you. You are all
bones and controlled dry grief.
In your conversation
there is only one sentence.
If she . . . it begins.

2: Backwards

Three years ago we walked together on the cliffs
at Onaero. I was six months gone
anguished and calm by turns. Your wife
was at home snapping and creaking
like pack ice. We walked on the cliffs
it was sunset you counselled me (old
friend old lover confidante) and your wife
shrieked like a harpy from the eye of the wind.
Later when we got back there was a quarrel.
Next morning the casuarinas applauded
silkily as I climbed into the car
the geese honked the goat capered
up and down the length of her chain.

3: Light

And here it is   Wellington
ahead to port
        a string
of beautiful lights around a black
                        vacancy

tiny concentric diamantes bracelet

the hills' wrists
            a single
filmy cloud floats like suds
in a bathtub
            below
our extended eager wheels.

Four hundred miles away
it is also night. By now
he will have stopped working
and begun to cook. There will be
Concert Programme Chopin on the radio

and a pool of light will
                        fall
through the open door
                  across
                              the veranda
and into the dark garden.

O quam gloriosum

In the absence of anything more than this, a figure
in a blue shirt crossing a street in sunlight
whom I may wave to in passing, who may
smile and draw no attention by it
I fill the house with Victoria — 'O quam
gloriosum' — those delicious cadences. Listen:
this waiting is a silence filled with music,
mere absence is an antiphon, an 0 flowering
into a melisma. ' "No" is easy, "yes"
more difficult,' you said, allowing the word
to hang suspended. So will you anticipate release;
the month will end, absence be filled, the sus-
pension will resolve. In that hard answer, yes,
do wanting and circumstance most gloriously concord.

Writing

I could have written, 'I left
you standing in the street;
it was dawn; the northwest arch
promised wind of the mountains'

— but this is hindsight. Or I
could describe it, how the light
fell on the land, and the land lay
under it, beautiful and meaningless.

But in fact I stared
out of the window most of the time
and tried to write. Five hundred
and ten miles an hour is a good

clean quick way to exit in anyone's
language. The writing on the wing
said REVERSE THRUST LEVER but I can't
see anyone getting out there at that speed.

'it, then'

& from that time we pull
away up into the light August and difficulty
lessens as we assume the old lives protectively
coloured and shapely enough & if it weren't for all
these journeys we insist on making
or get language to do for us the evasions
'it' 'then' as though something was and isn't un-
stuck so uncouple & loosen this clenching

& when you are 'home' again *Muntreal*
staring back at here fisheyed by distance
where jasmine sprawls over tin fences
fingering in the dusk the airs of Parnell
Road scent solid as the Abels factory recall
this one running and running on Museum Hill

Several ways of looking at it

i

It is a disease
not so much the twin tumescences
yours first mine later accompanied
by groans or shouting *keep quiet*
but its unpredictable course once infected

ii

how we have lurched in and out of
various states like drunks in a big hotel
Desire Ballroom with its twinkly lights slippery
allure Self-Reproach Cafe
Recrimination Suite Accusation Dining Room
the two elevators Hope and Despair go all the way
in only one direction Hope all mirrors and glitter
carried us to adjacent rooms on a cheap upper floor
Despair unlit all the way back
down to these dingy vacancies
I now inhabit
since you checked out & stand
at the corner of Third and Lethe *hush they'll*
hear

iii

though it's a plot from a quickie best-
seller offering foreign locations explicit
sex *keep quiet* passion great
dialogue and pace suitable for magazine
condensation e.g. page
thirty seven 'Oh my darling girl,' he said
page seventy eight 'Come as soon as you can'
page one forty three 'Hush, keep quiet or they'll
hear us' page two oh nine 'I don't want you to
come' the question being whether she'll get
what she wants & will he tell the grandparents
and how will it end if there is an ending
or just more reversals MORE NEXT WEEK

iv

or perhaps it is something else entirely
an illustration exemplum meaning morall
tale through fortitude in adversity or
fidelity or patience are discounted lines/
no demand for it nowadays/constancy
etc goes better with pointy archways and good
acoustics *keep quiet or they'll hear us*

v

one kind of silence
is indistinguishable from another
as judged by the measurable data
whatever occasions it

vi

the skies here you'll recall resemble
a bland flat-blue pudding basin inverted
over the city reducing windspeed (rarely
10 mph) and disturbing external influences
on some mornings the volcanic cone
cleaves bright water to shore up the sky
there's no more than three months between
leaf fall and sap rising
they all say it's a great
place to raise children in
you've said it yourself
keep quiet keep quiet or they'll hear you

vii

after the big explosion there is
such a silence
& out of it walk two people a woman a
small child they seem confused even dazed
they look at each other at the wreckage
and do not speak.

An evening in November

Eight hundred of them, and this as ordinary
as any. A sea breeze worries at the windows,
sunlight illuminates Rangitoto's flanks,
and in the next room, unimaginably, my son
sleeps in a basket. Seven days ago
he was still tucked inside; we were
bean and bean-pod, egg and egg-shell
a bellyful of rare fruit. Then
my son who was once an axolotl
once a little fish leapt
into his own life. His lungs
ballooned, his heart closed up,
his clear eye fixed mine, his fist
grasped my finger. As if it were
an ordinary day the sun rose.

Photographs for Daddy

1: Addition

After 10 weeks of it
you've done 700 nappy changes
in a ratio of 4:1 dirty
545 feeds of which 95
were at night
plus, if you're at all forgetful
there were 400-odd
sicked-upon shoulders.

But there's the blind
head butting the breast
and pulling down oh greedy
his first great milky gulps
till it spurts — and how he
purrs then
and leaves off half-
done to watch you oh eyes
oh sparrow mouth.

2: Abstraction

If mama is the word
babies make
with mouth and breast
it's father that's abstract
pure invention —
handy I suppose for opening
and closing doors
yet you can do it
with less fuss without.

3: Explanation

When an old fool at a party
says, 'Congratulations — when
did you get married?' say
you don't need to these days
and when he asks, 'But who's
the father?' with as much grace
as a lawyer in a paternity case
rehearse a few quick answers
any one of four — I don't know which
the test was inconclusive
don't tell the truth *whose*
damn business is it anyway?

4: Photographs for Daddy

Here you see
little round eyes
here his sparrow mouth here
his perfect feet
but the special smell of him
his warm head
the sounds he makes when joyous
these I cannot send
these you must come home for.

Parts of speech

There's that word again.
It would be funny if it weren't
sinister: the prisoner's word
for the gaoler. You can hear unremitting
violence behind the verb — a dull bang
some repetitive thumping, a few
gasps and a silence.
But this is not a political poem.

Consider this: object, about
three inches long, with a slotted top.
The whole material world revolves
(you could say) around it.
Harmless, even domestic. Nouns, you see,
can be relatively safe,
and this is not a political poem.

Gerund: make a thing out of doing.
If this is a metaphor it's skewed — hammering
nails would be closer to the bull. Teapots/
icing sets/forcing bags/garden hoses or if it must
be tools then an impact driver is more accurate:
ITEM 1 old lady ITEM 1 two-year-old ITEM
'domestic violence' ITEM snufflicks ITEM 'give
her what she deserves'.

But this is not a political poem.

The evader's cookbook

After a couple of hours in the boozer
you phone to cancel dinner — they're

old friends. 'Something has come up,' you say,
'I'd never get there.' An hour's drive. Anyway

she seems interested, so you invite
her back to your place for a bite.

'Come back to my lair,' you offer. 'I could
cook a spot of dinner.' There's been no food

in the place for months, but that's beside the point.
'Lair' was fair enough. Warning for those who want

to heed it. She comes, of course (you drive
her) and sits on your floor reading Gore Vidal

and laughing, while you slip upstairs to attend
to the sheets. Later you ask, 'What do you want

for breakfast?' 'What I had for dinner.'
'I'll put it in the microwave.' She giggles.

Embarras de plaisir

April's a waitress with pink hair
('She calls it apricot') but May
is an improvement, an eighteen year-
old secretary ('But she's nearly

nineteen') and after she's
filed there's a dancer who leaves
her clothes in his wardrobe
without asking. She'll have to go.

She's too keen anyway, proposes
marriage late at night, phones
him at the office. Far too soon
for that; thirty-five's too young

to start going steady. The problem
if there is one isn't quality
but there have been eight of them
already this year and it's only July.

In absentia

The problem is how to occupy dead
time. When some women weep, or drink,
or blab, take baths, go to pieces, read,

she finds herself making the most futile
of female gestures: washing the floors,
cutting flowers, dusting, setting all

to rights, as though what mute time shoves
aside or buries crumb by crumb can ward
off misfortune, is efficacious

against misery. It is mere cave
magic, does not rise above wax and water
or preclude snappishness, ill-temper

with small children; of virtues
it is the most insignificant. Of course
she would prefer, if she could choose,

to screech and wail like Ariadne, or hack
like Gaea at his balls. Instead she's meek
as a housewife ironing in a clean kitchen.

Michele Leggott

moons up
over afternoon gothic
in delta

orca mountains
rise east
west plainly from

canty polders
returning
american barns

skinny wind bands
pintails under
a distant eye

and later centric
wash rocks just
off the point

what was it
the ten of spades
face down

Yellow Pencil

the tides tip themselves
on their heads
week and week
                about

bright   clean   particular
but nothing hard about it

just the way things go

fuchsias
wine-dark (there it is)
in a blue

plastic

bucket

play of veranda
palings
and the depth beyond
them
     growing

nearly a year old
this:

it's good living
below fuchsia flowers
    brilliant divers out of the dark
    green feet first and coming down

how much
of the wording recurs
though we've changed
houses

white whales on the water
under the bank
or mangrove flats

play   or mud
depending on the week

don't explain

your peculiar charm
(that quick view)
against the downroad

each working morning

move across
to the other window

to be shown

bright marigolds
pink petunias
a row of buckets

and the negative field
exhilarating
between the palings

oh   hydrangeas
move compactly about
out front

deploy themselves
in tireless arrangements
of three

conspicuous for no reason
but the time of year
bunchy flowers to the ground

daleks

remove the clowns

what you're looking for
is the dark
              green

its promise of depth
(feet first)

in which to get every week
how you want it

reflecting white whales?

sure

and the white magnolia
and the fig tree in fruit
scented pelargonium
bougainvillea

more fervent perspectives

on a wish for movement

Watermelon World

she sings fish are jumping
in your room birds ride

around the walls pink is
picking up the white cotton

is high diamonds rose and
why one of these days

the picture may be painted
melons sent flying hearts

and stars harm nothing you
care about more than today

Wind Water

know where they
go and her
there going when

and even how
they do so
long after the rain

the blow
takes ('with beauty')
a bright push

has them
fall spicule
in the sun

Road Music

Just when you think you've made it
out of the bosom

you go back alone
your child asleep in the back

and the road is jammed with ghost Peugeots
grinding over the Mahoenuis
cornering with you in the gorge
                                    the stories burgeon
flying along the coast   the parallel track
a two-tone blast at the top of Mount Messenger

brief dark of the tunnel
where the clock turns over

Coming and going the ghosts travel with you
they overlay your rest

it's her voice calls your child in the pissy Ladies'
at Te Kuiti (Teka Witi)
his red sweater your jersey
your kiss her Kodachrome lipstick
(she hated the song)

the milkshakes are daylight robbery   the car plants groves
of plumstone trees   the seats go down
at night and the shorter child sleeps on the driver's side
the cabbages fell off the truck they said

at this corner   the very elegant coast of the northern bight
is Monterey   your father is the best driver
in the world
            coming or going
            how we would have driven that coast

your watercolour eyes make it into the scrub in time

a bird wekas off the road with inches to spare
a miss is as good as a mile

This time the white Peugeot
gets there with the rain and tails Datsuns
freighting kids home from winter term
or music lessons
                  the barley broth is in its third day
boiled clean of its bones   thick
with orthodoxy the spoons dredge up and convey
to mouths that have learned a rich language
of gristle and fat

you go out for tea and miss
this last detail of what is utterly familiar

will your boy thank you
for any of this?
            did you thank them?

or Beryl and Pat and Joyce
who feed you both and put up with his eighteen months?

You come back loaded with grapefruit, jam, corned beef
a case of green wine
                  and all the letters you wrote from years ago

(One) at a Time

red columbine walk
yolk sun tempera

dreamt a full rhyme
coming under an empty

year end I'm spoke
tell her one line—

'fall spicule' fool
setting to terms

spike lavender the
love cool invincible

An American Autumn

scripting

I would have met you there

it would have been at the invitation
of one or other
of us
        first had wit to hold out
        for coffee

and suggest lunch   I couldn't
have let you walk away
                        nor I you

beginning

a long order of maybe

cheese and chicken sandwiches
with lettuce and coffee
as always before
                never till now
                a million times since

September through September   you
wouldn't have let that go
                                me neither

wondering

why it all tasted so rare

I remember especially the kissing
crusts that thick
crockery
            with the crimson trim
            not cheap it's catering

supply she told us   but you can't
break it either I said
                        you grinned

Calligraph
        a character
            meaning
                tangle   wood
a scribble   of limbs
    rocking
            rubbing
            in the light spring
                        evening

strokes
        elbows
                oh buds
    here you come

& the complete   figure
        shoots up
                        loaded
            alight

            a tulip tree

white sky
vanilla rim
mountains

rake ginger
trash under
trees avenues

tastes sweet
difficult
on the tongue

see though
gone thinning
air 'bouton

boutonnière :
everything
flowers' that

old was sung
walks hard
around it

on white you fall
into line
          her voice fills
the ground
potato cuts
            the sun
dries paints
            the deck prints
shapes shadows
of oranges
          green
          'cyan and
          magenta'
                    sail
     your picnic

sea
   into the eye
   land crimson
   lemons
       hand me
the moon
risen rode
       rose ride
white
   out to see

Rose 4

there's
dwarf bramble
all over
      Alouette
mountain
      in August
             ah
             gentle
                gongle
             air
             for
              jangles
             raven
             jokers
                gentils
                jongleurs
paired airs'
zenith

Rose 6

saw oregon
       grape bloom blueberry
       maillot
   my eye

bayou
>saw fat bunches
>wrap
>>so
>>>delightedly
blue blue blue
no rose but the apple
>>>>my eye
>>>ripple
watched that tree
spring wind
>>counting time to
>>time from
>>>>Tydeman wind
>>>>falls early
>>now

Rose 7

and then
more comes
>>>prune plums bloom
>>>blue in the leaves
plum under the blue
bloom
>>prunus
>>>>spaces
the sky came through
saying
>>the dark leaves
>>open
>>>summer's
>>>catalogue
we began
keeping
>>and can't
>>finish

Elizabeth Nannestad

Stone Figure

Some medieval
simple soul in stone
holds the church roof, the weight
grown into his shoulders.
Fear of something or other
handles him, he
is twisted, looking back.
Little woman little man
the blackbirds of panic seize upon you
year after year
and build their rickety
shit-streaked nests in your hair.
You're gripped by the scrag.
You stay there.

Queen of the River

Here the boat set me down, and I wait. The oarsman swung on
the pole
and we came to the bank, lifted my belongings, and I got out.
Four days and five nights, the canoe does not return.
I waited at the river bank. Oh, the river. How I wept, and now
how dry I am.
                    This is only a tributary, and a thousand miles to
the sea,
a lifetime to the other side. The river bends, or is it that my eye
bends what I see with distance and time.
                                        The military walk in the
town.
The old giantess behind her stand in the market refuses to
bargain
selling fallen fruit smelling of diarrhoea, golden and black.
She looks down. The tiny captured monkeys
tethered to her, they also look down.

In the evening I walk to the river, at the end of town
and I watch the sun set in equatorial calm.

I see the circles on the slow-swift stream
and I hear the monkeys scream. It is all one.
I walk back to my hammock and lie down.

Opposite in the street is the tailor's shop, a carbox with an open
side
where the tailor works through the night. In the evening
his family comes and sits with him, a laugh breaks, and one sings
out.

Outside my room the night has turned to flowers. The tailor's
daughter
lines up her back with the side of the shop, looks down the
street.
The military drift, looking in at bars.

                              I am the queen of the River
and I go as I please. The river is as wide as this arm of mine,
I reach out and measure the river with my arm and touch on the
far side.
I will leave now. Why should I not go down?
A mosquito steps on my arm and clings.
My arms are bitten by the dark bougainvillea
and ignored by the spines.
                              I am the Queen of the
River,
and I know by now the one song they play, over and again,
down in my throat I know them, all the songs to this hour in
time
and I will drive the oarsman mad.

The tailor's little daughter kicks a foot at midnight.
It is cool now, and I who have flown in my dreams and died
stop sweating, pull the sheet up onto a shoulder, and sleep.

Mosquito

Ho, you there, little monster of depravity,
lift those hind-
quarters on my arm.

Are you finished? Been satisfied?
Well then, let's be
strangers.

Andean Flower

In one part of the journey, the mountain side
was charred, and a mist came down
that wet my hair against my face,
we could scarcely breathe.

I saw this one flower by the path
and I thought: That is my despair

Soon there were thousands of them
up and over the sides of the mountain.

The Altiplano

Who knows the altiplano? Who's been there?
No-one breathes the air of pure silver
and stays steady. Living on spit-beer and corn
no-one there lives long.

There are the thin dogs running and the thieves
by walls eroded by rains, and the sun
and the writings on the wall say:
Sing me a song of New Freedom.

Mother of mothers, whose eyes shine
what is she saying, on her knees in prayer
to her nailed saints in their niches?
Three hundred candles are weeping. Offer one.

Whoever flies over the altiplano and looks down
sees red backs scored, and the white road
drawn out around and over them, a signature
by an inventive hand.

We Watched the Moon Rise

We watched the moon rise
above the line of mountains.
The night was ice and sharp stars
and we shivered, my head on your shoulder.
We waited until the moon
was fully come, large and yellow
then went to our beds
and the moon
took the short way
around and went back down.

Lovesong in Front of Mountains

Look what you have done to me, once a wild, wild woman
running like the wind on the sea, not one way, but everywhere
Look at me. It's your voice has made me still.
We are in front of mountains.
Your hand is on my side
we hardly speak. Small birds come
quite near, to our feet
and call to each other, carrying clear on the cold, burning air.

You point out one among the mountains
and translate for me its name: "We have no guests here".
The late sun
runs red in my hair. It is yours, it is yours. Take it or leave it
until you deck my head with flowers
and sit me like this to look at mountains, and I am burned.

You Must Be Joking

I waited for you until the hours turned to stone
I came as agreed, you left me alone.

Now you have lost the expression
of furious impatience you saved for me:

"I had forgotten you were so gentle"

Oh then I loved you like the sun

But that was then, my friend, and now
By my ambition and my family name

By the brother I lost and the will I own
By the wind there on the street where I stood

You can call, you can call. I will not come.

What Makes the Heart Stand Still —

The winds of chance blow nightly, they blow away
the dirt and tears, and catch in the arms of trees.

It's a fine clear night. There's a high wind
beats up in the trees. Where else
could it be beating?

Patterns on the Floor of the Pool

Swallows, swallows
lit by the water shine.
First there are two,
now they are gone.

I cast my bread out onto the waters.
Why? Aren't you hungry?

I show the water how strong are my arms,
swim to the centre of the pool
stand up and look around.
I'm searching.
Where have they got to now?
Will they be long?

You ask too much. Look at you
still asking.

This small art

is nothing but
a long thorn
in my heart.

Take it. Go on.
You might not get
another one.

Come Back Down

Just sitting, thinking
on nothing in particular
the chair leg broke and left me

up in the air, thinking
upon a chair.

Jump

The water says, Come Here
and I say, No. You're
rough and wet and I'm fully clothed.

I'll stay on this rock
forever, if need be
and live on rock oysters

Too late. After all I do love to be
christened from head to heels
make my cold arms in the cold sea warm,
strike out for the shore.

Susan Allpress

Everywhere People Are Falling Asleep

wisps of people not quite forming   in rooms
of houses in high places   grey skys with
strings of light anchoring clouds   bouyant
as helium   balloons drinking tea from brightly
enamelled cups on rich carpet   there is fear
in the eyes of the girl with the red tutu   she
runs through the blossoming orchard scratching
her bare eczema'd arms on the lichen covered branches
      floating into the grey-white light blood
streaking the sky she dissolves a new picture forms
      fluffing up the pillows of a motel room   she has
married her father   the sap in the blue gum trees
threatens to stop   the leaves are synonyms for anxiety
      at the counter where the travel tickets are arranged
the vendor of escapes wants her for his own inward
flights   the design on his face melts   his skin
drips pale brown   his mask of cellophane ignites
      she sits on the worn wooden pew in an empty
sunfilled church

'A Kind of Alaska'

there are some things one can't
look up   tried an old friend
lately   gone away   a kind of
alaska   the top of the map not
much   up past there —
having things left to look up
a good enough reason to keep
on looking
write a   'look up book'
keep the world   t/k icking
always something to look
forward / up   to
ticking   who said that?
time is about to go off

that's what it read
last time I looked it up
Alaska   another set of bombs
slower   t i c k s
are you following this?
till there's nothing left
to look up

no adds

no reds

no addresses

no skirts

just Alaska

t i c k i n g

'Anti-Pornography' Poem — Finally
take a closer look next time
I'm undressing by the dusky window-light

    that moment she pauses
    arms above shoulders
    hair in mid-flight to back
                bare breasted
    she pauses to track black
    branches veining the even sky

take another look
focus the light
angle perspectives

inhale
  sweat-sweet
      freckles   hairs   dust
           the curves
come / go
      unhinge her from the page

more remote than fiction

the hour eats itself up
before any real snare
for truth is set

most of the time
it's not possible
to pin down

a fly is a fly is a fly
a fly in amber
      is a dead fly

to be specific /
the wind shifts & shifts
         & still shifts
& is always familiar

on thursday you put out the garbage
on friday you tear up old drafts

& loosing your head on saturday night
         you understand
there is no 'high order' of waste

and the place where they carve
from human bone a flute
is more remote than fiction

Janet Potiki

for a father in hiding
take me away
i used to travel.

i hear the breath of the people
in each corner
and scraping at the glass.

someone must have sent the dreams
of meeting houses
low and dark,
earth floors
and slits for windows,
each old face watching silently.

and i am searching, searching,
for the smallest entrance.

blind horses
scent the air
that blows through you.

the present
it wasn't really a nautilus
some shiny sea egg
a sac
pear full and fragile.

flaying fish cast your smokey rims
and breast milk pallor.
a hot fusion pouring into the ocean.
you came from a cold-blooded mating
into warm hands
that passed you to a womin
whose nose fits perfectly into yr orifice,

changes her
to a hawk without wings.

beauty cascading through opalescence

sea and air.

Tarawera

all i wanted was a tree
and a burning,
a hot stripping of the senses.

lift the shroud from the mountain,

basalt and iron
ferrous slit of the earth,
thick lipped ancestor.

scoria and dust
a red blister biting.

a womin plants a whenua
skin to skin
in black and white
a return to the source.

a gull flips,
over the valley
spagnum absorbs
the shocks
slow steps
rocking on the slopes
a procession
a movement
out
over the rim
a slide, a fall,
pouring to the bottom.

masked in chalk
walking on powder
the make-up of the mountain.

clean channels/direct passage
up the face,
one of many,
racking the shadows.

stone facts
panels drop.

in sun —
one man,
sleeps on her flanks
a solid embrace.

rods connect
hammers and tapes
record a response
live needles press, in sleep —
skin that burns
on waking.

hold tight
grip, till knuckles bleach — translucent
giving everything
back/to bone.

there's new blood on the mountain.

palazzi

sitting out on the palazzi
with my back to the open lounge
my lowered lids let the shine in.

a white porcelain bowl, used each morning,
the only religious ceremony left today — break fast,

an old one from the testaments.
it came from a rubbish dump at Kohukohu.

saw an Italian sun and thought about fast cars on the slopes.
red cars'n long scarf wommin. a trip on the grey gravel of
Europe.

i'd wear me blue dancing shoes and take me
fishes eyes.
daydreams on a cracked concrete slab in Rotorua.

cycle of five poems

Sulphur

A full breast to the moon
misty sulphur beats around the candle flame
and submerged in grey silk
I stretch full length and keep afloat.

Outside the pool I feel the full weight of you inside me,
still alive.

Inside the flat is a bed and a book.

Ika

My stomach is pulled tight now
heavy sand, before the tide
breathing is difficult.

Gasping fish swim past enormous rocks
and out to deeper water.
The little passage grows large
then closes again.
Ika does not look back.

Beached mucus dries and is returned to the land.
The little ika swims harder.

For Tarawera
Out of the shadows
out of the gloom
it was a rare rolling baby
eyes cast wide
Magic Magic, ferns 'n hot tides
Magic Magic, fishes eyes!

Late nights with baby
You bloody try writing at 3am
with a baby on one breast, and biting.
A pen in my left hand, stumblegaited it to the toilet.
Sitting beneath an unsubdued light
emblazoned, red-eyed and breathless
a blank, bleary beauty.

Babies sleep
Babies sleep
babies sleep
he dreams all the things he'll ever be.
Hands touch the night
lightly, lightly
he's asleep.

Chérie Barford

Plea To The Spanish Lady

*The people of Western Samoa were told that the sickness which eventually
killed twenty-two per cent of their population after World War One was called
'The Spanish Lady'. This is one man's plea.*

Important streets fall before you
and now   Talune berthed in Apia
harbours your sway
Sway not our way   Lady
Such homage grieves us

Aboard Talune the Doctor examines
bodies propped by mail bags
Colonel Logan agrees
                              'Yes,
a sea-sick lot this one.'
The ocean is calm

Today the Samoan Times is all news:
death notices and a front page
Today the editor died
Today Teuuila's screams awoke me
as she lay between her parents
dipping fingers in their sweat

Her name means flower   Lady
see her tremble and wilt
We will bury her in lavalava
scented with frangipani

At Papauta Girls' School desks are empty
Colonel Logan shouts 'I do not care if they
are going to die. Let them die and go to Hell.'
American medicine is sent back unopened

He's never cared for us   Lady
He's not my brother in Christ   He can't be
Logs tumble, tumble from his eyes

Crosses bearing corpses swim in them
My flesh is moist   too moist
Who will harvest the taro and breadfruit?
Who will instruct the young? Feed my children?

Don't linger Spanish Lady
The trenches are full and
my family spills into the ocean
fevered and dazed
drowning at each others' feet
go now   Lady
We have fallen before you

Today It's Wednesday

It was Thursday
when the Pope chastised
a Patagonian painter
and Friday
when rice pointed through
my colander towards the drain
like a short-grain army

I remember the days
because on Saturday I said
'flute my bones with melody brother'
and you ran on Sunday
wanting to know if I meant anything
or was just being dramatic

I sent you rice and sunflower seeds
cellotaped into an unsigned card
on Monday
which you'd have opened on Tuesday
and today it's Wednesday and raining

Lubeck Castle

Leaning across the rack
to ask for hours
                and minutes
my naval pressed
against polished wood

For an instant
time stretched
into waves of storks
arriving and departing
above a thawing Baltic

Past/ present/ future blurred
as my mind
                still intact
fled the room

Cylindrical Sleeve

Based on a painting 'The Maries At The Tomb' at Auckland Art Gallery

Sunday afternoon/ McCahon's
angel points intent with
message
        from the back wall

Mary gazes into his sleeve
— seeking/ finding comfort
in the fabric's curve   but

I turn from that finger
jabbing direction thru humid air
                towards a

bearable horizon
            of trees
                arching into heaven

Jenny Bornholdt

Rodnie And Her Bicycles

You and all your bicycles
coming down out of the sky like
wheeled birds, coat flaps
like wings
           I like to think of you and them
           pedalling through the sky
           each revolution a small turn
           elsewhere.

You only ever wanted
one
you said, but they seemed to
seek you out
each morning dawned a new bicycle.

Now you have two in the shed
           a new blue one to ride
           one in the cupboard
           and the old black one which you put
out to pasture in the garden
in between the new plants.

I like to think of you
and the bicycles — all those possible
journeys waiting in cupboards
and behind old doors and,
in the night, you cycling out
through the garden,
your face shining like the spokes
from all your bicycles,
joy spinning in your face
like a wheel.

You

I keep writing poems
that skim over the top of you
like herons over still water.
What is true
is that you have
a space in my head
all of your own
I hold you there
in thin arms
feel your heart
kick in time.

Sitting on a red bus

Sitting on a red bus
this afternoon I
started thinking about
you for no obvious reason
but it was probably started
by that magazine picture of
a young man's smooth back
with his shoulderblade
slicing like a beautiful knife
through the page and
although I never saw your
back bare, or touched clear
skin, the thought was there
once or twice —
a smooth handed notion which
shrugged itself off to safer
places and all the time you
probably knew it was
that other one who
really turned my head
— eyes that wanted climbing
into, but I never ventured there
and when he hugged me that time
saying 'yes I'm fine'
I wanted him to come up from

the depths and wanted to say:
don't lie
your shoulderblades slice into my palms
don't pretend
they cut shapes like children's cutouts
unfolding endlessly

Scrub cut

I

These hairs like
fern fingers
curl on my arm
dropped there during
the tree felling
the scrub cutting
the letting in of light.

You have trimmed away
the undergrowth
making way

There is now no saying
'That is Manuka.
That is Rimu.
Look, there is a Pohutukawa
that will have red flowers
of this particular shade,
with the needles falling.'

II

This bristly crop
tells of nothing but
beginnings.
Here it is, here I am
grinning out at you from
this big face.

Whale

My father is a whale.
I want to save him
from extinction.
He walks out into the waves
with his hands
on his big hips
I want   to learn the lingo
trace the salted slipstreams
of blue journeys
swim with the sleek sides gentle roll
find   why the death beach?
          why the dying mounds of sighing bodies?
cry   save the whale/s.

Miles

'Miles, you've got to come in now'

'Miles we've got to come in now'
      (A smaller voice)

running in from
playing hide and seek
among the parked cars
sleeping sharks
almost dark

come in Miles

your mother waits
arms nursing folded sheets
like package deals

come in Miles
the light's going
down the street.

Eavesdrop on a Taxi Radio

In the taxi
came the names
of all the streets
I have ever lived in
people wait on all
the corners
you were there
on every doorstep.
Now we drive past houses
thrown flat
on the hillside
like dark palms
there are no doors for you
to wait at
you would stand there
knocking on green grass.

A Love Poem has Very Long Sentences

'This is a sort of love poem
it has some long sentences
one in particular is very long.'

That is because there can be a lot to say
in a sort of love poem
sorting out the sort of from the is, for instance
trying to get it all down
for example: the silent blue of water
            the sound of fallen leaves on a bare throat
            the movement of trees
            the dissolve of skin on skin
            the crack of thin white bones

there is a lot you can say in a
sort of love poem
it probably helps to have some long sentences
and there is nothing to be ashamed of
in having one in particular that is very long
like you said, if you stick with it you will probably get to
the end eventually.

Poem

So far
it has worked
by imagining you
in all the places I would
like you to be

★

this is the one I love.
he is not here
but the air is still warm
from where he
might have been

★

we have spent hours
circling each other
with words — thinly
vowelled embraces

how to translate these
words into silences
or the silences
into words

★

when I cannot fix you
behind my eyes
I carry your absence
like stars
on the blue roof

'In the garden . . .'

In the garden
the bulbs run riot
root systems go
all over the place
we crack open huge dry
clods of earth and uncover
white bulbs of onion flowers
embedded like fossils
their roots like thin streamers
partying down through the soil.
So we have a white flower
propped on the top of a green stem
a plain enough thing
while underneath
the feelers are out
hooking into other systems
forming the network
the flower an undercover agent
posted on the watch
a decoy of simplicity.

Kim Eggleston

Sundown

Rex comes up the path
in the twilight thick
overhead bush

Across the lupin flats
the dump-fires burn like rags
surfers crash in the shipwreck waves

In the still smoke evening
the frogs are singing
the bamboo strikes its black

iron feathers into the air
He comes up the path
to the lighted window

and the last of the magnolia
is sweet as the tingle of frost
with milk for his tea

The coloured glass
around the front door
shines a rainbow shelter

The door swings
to his touch
the golden oaken hall

swallows him in
and the sun
is free to go.

Broad Bay

Sometimes when the light is slow down
the hill from the castle and the sea
is hammering at the heads

I walk across the hill
to where the albatross lives
and watch the sea bite the land

Sometimes when the light is slow
and the sea is flat
floundering in the mud

We wonder should we leave
or stay on the verandah and smoke
another cigarette

The fine net falls either way
as it does when you're arguing
about a jersey and you've

already got your coat on.

Fire Another Round

Your letter caught us
sitting on barstools
two women in linen suits
and flashing legs
It said something about
fire
destroyed the house
and all the trees about
for miles
and scars and bandages
priceless possessions
You were going away
for a while
and we wouldn't
hear from you
The letter smells black
smoke around the edges
and we are sitting on barstools
swinging our legs
round another round.

Wednesday Afternoon in June

The whole afternoon
smells of wet beech
and damp soil
Even when I light a cigarette
the smoke swings slowly
through the air
that hasn't dried all day
Good afternoon for walking
through old sawmills
smoking Mild 10's
Washing hung on the line
for a week
and the pale sun
shines luminous
through the barber's trailing ribbons
Good afternoon
to sit and let the rusting leaves
fall and slide, slide and fall
To catch beauty
in your throat,
cross your heart
and hope to live
And after tea
in the hour
between light and dark
fetching a box of wood
I hear the dog growling
and I look up the fence
and see him
A big man in a big coat
with a hat low on his eyes
standing there
watching the dog
still and silent as the big beech tree
a gun broken over his arm
He stands there
watching me
watching the dog
then he turns and crunches
down the road

Gone hunting
and the night closes
solid and damp
behind him.

If the body wasn't there

If the body wasn't there
but drank and danced
laid head on shoulder
slung hat at cocktail shirt
flashed a finger at schoolgirl skirt
If body wasn't there
but wrote letters like it was
and farted in the breakfast chair
watched it drink a lot of beer
said flowers and cuddling make you queer
told everyone it wasn't fair
and ate its dinner on the carpet stair
If the bloody body wasn't there
and you'd lied to me for half a year
all my love is hated.

No Goodbye

Are we in love
I can't remember
if we are fighting
with cold sour faces
or in love
with a cuddle by the sink
while I lay on the floor
covering shit
froth smothered and sweat
My face ripping up
like it's had a stroke
Mashing and groaning
on the doorstep to die

Where's my kid
and all the work to be done
The bastards I liked
and never told them so
The ones I didn't
and did tell them so
And where are you
through the haze of my fear
My body releasing its hold
altogether
I can't see you
And I'm going now, gone

He tells me next day
in a hospital yawn
Miners and their wives
don't fight in the morn
You never know if he's coming back.

She didn't like me wearing

She didn't like me wearing
her dead lover's clothes
Coming through the half-night
like an overdosed ghost

Her shop had a jukebox
the best mustard sauce you'd ever eat
Artfull paintings on the wall
and I cracked in dead on his feet

I knew he had died
but not that she was his
But his brother gave me the clothes
and blood is thicker than piss

She turned away when I ordered a steak
a victim of junkie romance
Second to the needle, holes in her eyes
True, they're a great pair of pants.

Index of Titles and First Lines

Titles are in *italics*; first lines in roman.

220   INDEX